Cambridge Elements ≡

Elements in Anthropological Archaeology in the 21st Century
edited by
Eli Dollarhide
New York University Abu Dhabi
Michael Galaty
University of Michigan
Junko Habu
University of California, Berkeley
Patricia A. McAnany
University of North Carolina at Chapel Hill
John K. Millhauser
North Carolina State University
Rita Wright
New York University

ANTHROPOLOGICAL ARCHAEOLOGY UNDERWATER

Ashley Lemke
University of Wisconsin – Milwaukee

CAMBRIDGE
UNIVERSITY PRESS

CAMBRIDGE
UNIVERSITY PRESS

Shaftesbury Road, Cambridge CB2 8EA, United Kingdom

One Liberty Plaza, 20th Floor, New York, NY 10006, USA

477 Williamstown Road, Port Melbourne, VIC 3207, Australia

314–321, 3rd Floor, Plot 3, Splendor Forum, Jasola District Centre,
New Delhi – 110025, India

103 Penang Road, #05–06/07, Visioncrest Commercial, Singapore 238467

Cambridge University Press is part of Cambridge University Press & Assessment,
a department of the University of Cambridge.

We share the University's mission to contribute to society through the pursuit of
education, learning and research at the highest international levels of excellence.

www.cambridge.org
Information on this title: www.cambridge.org/9781009494649

DOI: 10.1017/9781009327367

First published 2024

A catalogue record for this publication is available from the British Library.

ISBN 978-1-009-49464-9 Hardback
ISBN 978-1-009-32733-6 Paperback
ISSN 2753-6327 (online)
ISSN 2753-6319 (print)

Cambridge University Press & Assessment has no responsibility for the persistence
or accuracy of URLs for external or third-party internet websites referred to in this
publication and does not guarantee that any content on such websites is, or will
remain, accurate or appropriate.

Contents

Anthropological Archaeology Underwater

Elements in Anthropological Archaeology in the 21st Century

DOI: 10.1017/9781009327367
First published online: May 2024

Ashley Lemke
University of Wisconsin – Milwaukee
Author for correspondence: Ashley Lemke, ashlemke@uwm.edu

Abstract: Anthropological archaeology underwater is a new field. What type of research is this and how do anthropologists go about it? When most people hear the phrase "underwater archaeology," they think of shipwrecks and dramatic images of lost ships at sea, but the underwater archaeological record is vast. In addition to historic vessels, water preserves some of the oldest landscapes on the planet. While archaeologists are interested in the past, those working underwater apply the latest technologies to provide fresh understandings about ancient human behavior. Underwater environments provide preservation that is unmatched on land and therefore the data collected are novel – providing information about human lifeways and creating a picture of the past we would otherwise never see. This Element will explore the world of anthropological archaeology underwater, focusing on submerged sites, and review the techniques, data, and theoretical perspectives which are offering new insights into the human story.

Keywords: underwater archaeology, submerged prehistory, anthropology underwater, prehistoric archaeology, SCUBA diving

ISBNs: 9781009494649 (HB), 9781009327336 (PB), 9781009327367 (OC)
ISSNs: 2753-6327 (online), 2753-6319 (print)

1 Introduction: Archaeology Underwater

Underwater archaeology is not a new practice, although it is important to distinguish the systematic investigation and analysis of cultural material found underwater, from shipwreck hunting, looting, treasure collecting, and marine salvage. Archaeology underwater is seen as dramatic, often fueled by harrowing stories of storms and shipwrecks, warfare, and plane crashes, while diving itself still has an adventurous allure. But beyond this perception of the field, what truly is underwater archaeology? Simply – archaeology underwater – the study of the human past through material remains in or adjacent to underwater environments. While we often think of underwater archaeology taking place in the oceans, submerged environments containing archaeological remains also include lakes, rivers, reservoirs, cenotes, swamps, and other drowned sites. While archaeology is the study of the past, we use the latest technology, and this is especially true given the challenges of working underwater and caring for waterlogged materials. Despite taking place underwater – it is still archaeology and as such can be rooted in anthropological theory. Situating archaeology underwater within archaeological practices and anthropological approaches in general is a main theme of this Element as well as introducing the vast array of submerged sites all over the world. Theoretical orientations, research frameworks, and methods will be discussed in Sections 2 and 4, but it is critical to note from the outset that underwater archaeology combines ideas and approaches from many disciplines, (anthropology and archaeology of course) but also history, geology, geophysics, geomorphology, paleoenvironmental research, paleoecology, seafloor and subsea technologies, robotics, SCUBA (self-contained underwater breathing apparatus) diving, and engineering. Due to the similarities between archaeology on land and archaeology below water, this Element will often use "archaeology underwater" rather than underwater archaeology (following Bass 1966).

Why are some archaeological sites submerged? How do they form? There are a range of different site types underwater, along a spectrum from some catastrophic event that sank a ship, or submerged an airplane, to those that were once terrestrial sites and have been drowned. Archaeological sites become inundated due to slower geological processes such as sea level rise, or faster geological processes, such as earthquakes and resulting land subsidence. Working in underwater environments can be challenging and may be expensive, so why do underwater archaeology at all? Beyond the fact that underwater or offshore settings are just an extension of the archaeological record, one that deserves to be investigated and protected in its own right, submerged environments offer some of the best preservation in the world, where limited oxygen and other factors often leave organic materials more intact than they would be on land. The waterlogged, anaerobic (the absence of free oxygen), and often anoxic (the absence of any oxygen) context of underwater settings preserves stone, ceramics, and other durable materials similar to terrestrial sites but also organic materials often missing on land, resulting in higher resolution archaeological data (Maarleveld 2020). Furthermore, some of the most important questions facing anthropology and archaeology today rely on data that are now underwater. Questions as far-ranging and diverse as human evolution, global human expansion, early seafaring, the origins of coastal adaptations, the movement of enslaved peoples, societal responses to climate change, and many others can be addressed by underwater archaeologists (e.g., Dunnavant 2021; Lemke 2021). Equally, the types of sites and data preserved underwater range from historical and prehistoric shipwrecks and canoes to sunken cites, submerged landscapes, human remains, and ritual or votive offerings. Essentially the full range of site types we know of from terrestrial contexts are also preserved below water, usually with higher data quality. Beyond that, underwater settings preserve some types of sites that do not survive on land at all – as underwater environments, especially those that are largely inaccessible, far offshore, and/or in deep water, are protected from postdepositional disturbances and subsequent human occupation. Types of sites and types of data are further detailed in Sections 3 and 5.

Overall, underwater sites offer significant contributions to our knowledge of the past. Individual ship and plane wrecks offer historical insights into technological development and provide accidental time capsules and details considering the circumstances of the event and the magnitude of loss of life. Submerged sites offer evidence that often does not exist on land, representing time periods and data that are not preserved in terrestrial settings, giving us additional insights into environmental adaptations and problem solving, the world's first mariners, and coastal use and colonization. For these reasons and others, the archaeological record underwater is an important part of our global shared history, which is protected by the UNESCO 2001 Convention on the Protection of the Underwater Cultural Heritage (hereafter, the UNESCO 2001 Convention, see Evans et al. 2010).

It is important that we first understand the history of archaeologists working underwater, to separate it from non-science on underwater sites, to outline various research trajectories, and finally to demonstrate the range of underwater archaeological projects. While a short review follows, underwater archaeology is often thought to be synonymous with nautical, or shipwreck archaeology, which is often conducted from a historical perspective with different research questions, scales of inquiry, and ultimate goals; after reviewing the history of underwater archaeology, this Element will focus primarily on submerged sites and landscapes and their investigation through an anthropological lens.

1.1 A History of Archaeology Underwater

Underwater archaeology as a discipline or subfield or specialty (it has been called all of these, see Section 2), had what can be characterized as a rocky start. It struggled to establish itself as bona fide archaeological research for several reasons. First, there are access and methodological difficulties in researching sites underwater, but second and more critically, some of the tools and skills used early on were developed by shipwreck salvagers. It is therefore critical to distinguish between what is and what is *not* archaeology underwater. Salvage, or the removal of materials for their monetary value, is not archaeology. Similar to looting on land, salvage is a notable issue in underwater archaeology, specifically for shipwrecks as many vessels were often carrying items of great value. After wrecking/sinking, depending on the context of the wreck (Were there eyewitnesses? Is the location of the wreck known? Is it in shallow water, areas of slow-moving currents, etc.?), materials may have been salvaged very quickly, similar to tombs being robbed in antiquity. Other wrecks are salvaged much later as they are discovered, or technology becomes available to access them. In all these cases, salvaged materials range from valuables including gold and jewels to warfare equipment such as cannons, and memorabilia such as bells, nameplates, or other items. Souvenir collecting is also not archaeology, the casual removable of materials for personal use, treasure hunting, or fortune and glory is also not archaeology. Lastly, snorkeling or SCUBA diving on shipwrecks is not scientific archaeology; divers sometimes collect souvenirs from wrecks and/or they impact a site and its archaeological integrity by moving objects to different places or by modifying the vessel itself, occasionally inscribing their names on it, like graffiti over rock art. While SCUBA diving on a wreck site is not archaeology, many SCUBA divers and their communities have worked closely with archaeologists to share site locations and conduct scientific investigations of sites (Scott-Ireton et al. 2023).

To trace the route from salvage to science, the history of underwater archaeology can be broken down into four phases: (1) 1600s–1960 Salvaged Treasure, (2) 1960–Present, Shipwrecks, (3) 1970s–1990s, Submerged Sites, (4), 1990s–Present, Deep Prehistory. The history of underwater archaeology has been covered elsewhere (see Broadwater 2002; Ford et al. 2020; Garrison and Cook Hale 2021), here the focus is to provide background as context for understanding the growth of the field, the various types of sites that exist underwater, the introduction of different methods for investigating such sites, and the origin of disciplinary divergences in underwater archaeology, which will be discussed in Section 2. These are chronological and developmental stages and within each, significant methodological leaps will be outlined and notable sites will be introduced. The history of archaeology underwater is the history of ideas and theories, the development of methods, and the history of actual discoveries.

The first period marks the earliest examples of salvage from shipwrecks and other artifacts recovered from underwater contexts. The second phase marks the first systematic archaeological research underwater by George Bass, and subsequently the birth of both nautical and maritime archaeologies (Bass 1966, 1971, 1988; Muckelroy 1978, see Section 1.1.2). During the third phase, submerged prehistoric sites were systematically excavated for the first time, and lastly, the fourth phase marks the deepest and earliest known artifacts to have been recovered from underwater contexts. Within each developmental stage, it will be clear that the history of underwater archaeology is intimately connected with the history of subsea research and technology in general (Broadwater 2002:17). It parallels trends in diving, bathymetric mapping, SONAR (sound navigation and ranging) technologies, and other improvements and draws extensively from them. Beginning with breath holding and then the use of diving bells in the seventeenth and eighteenth centuries, it wasn't until the twentieth century that the most well-known and common underwater breathing technique, SCUBA with self-contained gas, was used extensively. While vessel salvage using breath holding, diving bells, and surface-supplied air dates back centuries, the invention of the Aqualung in 1943, the first SCUBA system by Jacques-Yves Cousteau and Emile Gagnon, revolutionized research underwater. Indeed, the emergence of systematic underwater archaeology coincides with SCUBA becoming generally affordable in the 1960s and 1970s. Additionally, the large-scale commercial development of SONAR and other subsea equipment for accurate mapping led to the incorporation of these technologies into archaeological research (e.g., side-scan SONAR, magnetometer, sub-bottom profiler, multibeam SONAR, fathometer, global positioning systems, etc. see Section 4). Both the history of diving and subsea mapping technologies greatly influenced the development of underwater archaeology, and the gradual incorporation of these techniques is discussed below.

1.1.1 1600s–1960 Salvaged Treasure

Pioneering efforts to recover archaeological artifacts from underwater happened at least as early as the seventeenth century when divers using a bell recovered a cannon from the *Vasa* (or *Wasa*) warship in Sweden in 34 m of water (1663). Built between 1626 and 1628 *Vasa* foundered (or filled with water and sank) after sailing just 1300 m on its maiden voyage. Thirty-five years after its sinking, the first salvage operation took place. Other salvage operations also used open diving bells to salvage wreck sites in the Caribbean Sea (1685) (Broadwater 2002: 23). A Spanish ship the *Concepción*, grounded on a reef in 1641. Given the nature of the wrecking event, which included storms, drownings, starvation, and sharks, the remaining survivors could not report the location of the wreck accurately. After its discovery in 1685, Sir William Phips salvaged treasure from the wreck using an open bell at what was called Silver Shoals. Similar operations during the eighteenth century in England and Italy using diving bells and metal helmets met with minimal success but included the first underwater excavation (Broadwater 2002). In 1716, in England, William Tracey dove in a leather dress with a metal helmet while trying unsuccessfully to raise the wreck of the *Royal George*, a British ship, sunk near Portsmouth in 19 m of water. In 1775 Italy, the first underwater "dig" took place when English antiquarians sponsored an expedition to recover artifacts from the Tiber River using an open bell. In the nineteenth century, between 1839 and 1843 the *Royal George* was finally removed using Augustus Siebe's diving equipment. The enclosed suit and helmet system was developed in 1837 and is the forebear of hard hat diving systems. This dive was the first recorded use of the "buddy system" in diving and the wreck was blown up and salvaged. In 1854, the first archaeological diving team investigated the remains of prehistoric pile dwellings in Lake Zurich, these were the remains of stilt houses built on marshy land, raised to protect the houses against occasional flooding (Delgado 1997: 236–237). In the 1860s divers investigated the submerged remains of crannogs (artificial islands with dwellings) in Scotland (Morrison 1985: 4–6) and numerous Mesolithic artifacts were recovered and reported off the coast of Denmark in the Baltic Sea (Müller 1897: 18–23).

Throughout the twentieth century, there was rapid change and improvements in discovering and recovering materials from underwater archaeological sites. Many famous shipwrecks such as the *Antikythera* were discovered in the early 1900s by sponge divers in the Mediterranean (Muckelroy 1978: 12) and in 1900 in Greece surface-supplied helmet divers worked at 55 m to recover statuary from a Roman wreck carrying Greek art and were under the supervision of an archaeologist. Just 100 years later MIT's *Odyssey* autonomous underwater vehicle (AUV) was deployed in Greece to search for shipwrecks in the Mediterranean. Other notable events during the early twentieth century include 1909 in México when Edward Thompson recovered over 30,000 Mayan artifacts from the cenote at Chichén Itzá by lowering a bucket attached to a pulley system into the water. This was the first major underwater artifact recovery in the western hemisphere resulting in the discovery of gold, jade, and wooden figures, which were ritually deposited into the cenote (Coggins and Shane 1984; Lenihan et al. 2017). In 1927, Neolithic and Bronze Age pile dwellings in the

Swiss Lakes/Alps were seen on early aerial photographs (Stickel and Garrison 1988: 71). In 1931, the fishing boat *Colinda* recovered a mass of peat with a barbed antler harpoon point embedded in it off of Norfolk, among the first evidence of Doggerland, a submerged landscape that was dry land until ~6,000–7,000 years ago, which connected the United Kingdom to continental Europe (Martin 2020). In 1935, Jim the "Iron Man" Jarratt used a one-atmosphere diving suit to locate the *Lusitania* at 90 m. Between 1957 and 1961 in Sweden, after the cannon was raised in 1663, the *Vasa* itself was raised from 34 m of water and is regarded as one of the most significant and successful shipwreck recoveries of all time.

To summarize this first stage, from the 1600s to 1960, underwater investigations of archaeological sites primarily focused on salvaging treasure and/or valuables, in addition to locating wrecks of historical significance in deep waters. From a methodological perspective, it is clear that the history of underwater archaeology is connected to the history of diving. The incorporation and evolution of different diving techniques – from bells to one-atmosphere suits – were tied into both underwater salvage and archaeological discovery. Prior to the invention of the Aqualung and large-scale and affordable SCUBA gear, these incidental discoveries of underwater finds remained the extent of underwater archaeological research until 1960. Significantly these early finds already indicated that different types of archaeological sites were underwater, including shipwrecks where some catastrophe sank a vessel but also ritual deposits where artifacts were intentionally sunk, such as the figures in the Chichén Itzá cenote (Coggins and Shane 1984) and the river offerings in the Tiber, as well as evidence of architecture including pile dwellings and crannogs.

1.1.2 1960–Present, Shipwrecks

The break between the first and second stages in underwater archaeology as defined here is 1960. 1960 represents a significant shift in underwater interactions with archaeological sites going from discovering them, salvagers taking artifacts or entire ships to the surface, to systematic archaeological investigations. This stage is primarily focused on shipwrecks and systematic underwater archaeology emerged with a nautical focus on identifying, mapping, photographing, and excavating shipwrecks in the Mediterranean (Bass 1966; Bass et al. 1967; Bass and Van Doorninck 1982; Throckmorton 1970). Earlier campaigns include Cousteau's efforts to excavate the *Mahdia* shipwreck off the coast of Tunisia in 1948 where the Aqualung and airlifts were first used (Broadwater 2002), but it was in 1960 in Turkey that the first professional underwater archaeological excavation was conducted by Bass and colleagues in

29 m of water on a wreck dating to 1300 BC. This team would establish high standards for future underwater archaeological projects.

Bass' investigation of a fourth century Byzantine shipwreck at Yassi Ada, Turkey, is considered the first controlled excavation of an underwater site, with careful mapping of each artifact in situ and excavations in controlled layers, first recording and removing the cargo and then proceeding down to the hull planking. Underwater excavation techniques were invented throughout the course of this project, as the crew had to deal with some unforeseen challenges of working in an underwater environment. For example, each wooden piece of the vessel had to be secured to the sea floor using bicycle spokes so that each plank could be mapped before floating away. This early work established that controlled excavation was possible in underwater contexts using SCUBA gear that allowed archaeologists the flexibility they needed, and that intact ship-wrecks as well as scattered wreck sites could yield valuable data to historians, classicists, and archaeologists (Bass 1966; Gould 2000; Muckelroy 1978, 1980). Their research demonstrated that shipwreck construction and trade routes could be reconstructed in amazing detail by examining wreck sites. It also showed that virtually everything from tiny stone blades to huge temple columns were carried on the sea and much was lost in wrecking events, providing time capsules of the movement of goods. Archaeological research underwater could therefore gain unique knowledge of technology, art, and history from ancient cargoes. These early efforts were crucial for demonstrating that the systematic investigation of wrecks could provide details about the past we would otherwise never see.

From 1960 to the present, shipwreck investigations have offered a venue for technological development. Just as the history of diving is tied to the develop-ment of underwater archaeology, so is the evolution of subsea technology, including remote sensing cabled and towed instrumentation, submarines, remotely operated vehicles (ROVs), AUVs, and most recently unmanned, autonomous surface vessels (ASVs). 1963 was the first use of side-scan SONAR to find a shipwreck, developed by Harold Edgerton of MIT. 1964 was the first use of a submersible to map a shipwreck when Bass mapped an ancient wreck in the Mediterranean using the special-purpose submarine *Asherah* (named after the Semitic goddess "she who treads on the sea"). Submarines in archaeology have multiple uses including exploration and dis-covery of sites, documentation, and sampling, and can act as an aid for SCUBA divers. Specific wrecks were often the target of evolving methods as each site presented its own methodological hurdles. For example, the United States Ship (USS) *Monitor* and *Hunley* are famous American Civil War vessels. The *Monitor* was built in 1862 and was the first ironclad of the Union Navy. The

Hunley was built the following year in 1863 and was a Confederate submarine, the first to sink an enemy ship. The *Monitor* was discovered off Cape Hatteras in 1973, it was mapped in 1974, artifacts were recovered by divers in 1977, and in 1979 the deepest "hands-on" investigations by professional archaeologists to date took place in 73 m of water. Archaeologists also began incorporating subsea technologies such as ROVs into their expeditions. The first deepwater excavation with an ROV took place in 1990 for the Tortugas Project, where ROV *Merlin* worked on a Spanish shipwreck from 1622 in 457 m. The following year, ROV *Nemo* raised gold from the 1857 wreck *Central America* from 2,438 m.

Overall, this period marks many of the most important technological leaps for conducting archaeology underwater including the use of Aqualungs for flexible diving, the airlift for controlled excavations, the development of underwater photography and mapping techniques pioneered by Bass (1964), and lastly, the first use of side-scan SONAR to locate a shipwreck in 1963. Although submerged sites and shipwrecks were known for centuries, it wasn't until the culminating advent of all these tools, that archaeological research could be conducted underwater to the same standards as it was conducted on land.

1.1.3 1970s–1990s, Submerged Sites

Following close on the heels of the pioneering research of shipwrecks, archaeological sites which have been submerged due to changing water levels were known from at least the nineteenth century (e.g., Müller 1897: 18–23) and came to be systematically investigated for the first time in the 1970s. While limited excavations took place in the early 1970s, in the south sea of Funen, Denmark (Skaarup 1983, 1993), the first systematic, large-scale excavation of a submerged prehistoric site occurred from 1978 to 1988 at the site of Tybrind Vig (Andersen 2013). Tybrind Vig is located 300 m off the Danish coast in 3 m of water and is an extensive Late Mesolithic-Ertebølle cultural settlement with a radiocarbon date from a human burial dating the occupation to 6,400 cal yr BP. Mesolithic artifacts near the site (about 500 m south) were first located in 1957 by amateur archaeologists/SCUBA divers (Albrectsen 1959), and in the early 1970s when SCUBA equipment became generally affordable, systematic excavations were carried out in 1 x 1 m squares. Of the material remains excavated, close to 60 percent are organic, including a wickerwork fishing trap, components of fishing weirs, fishhooks made of red deer bone (one with a piece of a line attached), wooden fishing spear tines, textiles, three wooden dugout boats made of limewood, and wooden paddles made of ash, four of which are decorated (Andersen 2013; Malm 1995: 393, Figure 12).

Following Tybrind Vig, in numerous parts of the world, submerged site research emerged. Investigations included systematic survey and excavation of submerged sites in the Baltic, the Mediterranean, and inland Florida. Early survey with the help of a predictive model located additional submerged Mesolithic sites preserved in the slow-moving and shallow waters of the Baltic Sea off the coast of Denmark (Andersen 1980, 1987; Fischer 1995a). Similar to Tybrind Vig, these well-preserved sites have produced a wide array of architecture and artifacts including domestic structures, wooden objects, and textiles (Fischer 1995a, b). In the Mediterranean, underwater site surveys and limited excavation took place off the Carmel Coast of Israel. Sites here are 250 m off the coast in 1–12 m of water and are well preserved under sand. Occasional industrial dredging and intense storms exposed these sites anywhere from a few days to a few months and six were identified early on during these periods of exposure and surveyed (Galili and Wienstein-Evron 1985). These include Late Neolithic-Chalcolithic stone structures such as rectangular house floors, hearths, storage pits, and silos (dated to 6,830 cal yr BP) with lithic artifacts, basalt grinding slabs, ceramic sherds, limestone bowls, and bone fragments (Galili and Wienstein-Evron 1985). In Florida, a karstic landscape of rivers and sinkholes was explored early on by SCUBA divers. In Wakulla Springs divers recovered artifacts and fossils, while Little Salt Spring, Warm Mineral Spring, and the Guest Mammoth site saw excavations of archaeological materials in the 1970s and 1980s (e.g., Hoffman 1983).

The earliest prehistoric site which was found and explored in this period was Fermanville, a Middle Paleolithic occupation discovered in 1968, and excavated periodically during the 1970s–1980s. Originally discovered by petroleum geologists conducting geomorphological surveys, over 2,500 Mousterian lithic artifacts have been recovered near the base of a submerged granite cliff north of Cherbourg, France. This site has pre-served stratigraphy and demonstrates that Neanderthals were living 20 m below the present sea level at least 45,000 years ago (the site has been relatively dated based on geological evidence to 40–90,000 cal yr BP). Fermanville seems to present an ideal place for occupation, as Neanderthals living there could take advantage of the proximity to both terrestrial and marine resources, as well as local lithic raw materials (Scuvée and Verague 1988). Fermanville provided additional evidence of the prehis-toric occupation of Doggerland. The antiquity of the site was particularly important since it was the first submerged site dating to before the Last Glacial Maximum – demonstrating that archaeological sites and stratig-raphy could survive first inundation, then fully glacial conditions, and subsequent transgressions (water level rises) (Scuvée and Verague 1988).

This period revealed that the same techniques developed in terrestrial settings as well as those developed for shipwrecks could be combined and used to excavate prehistoric sites underwater. The use of predictive models in Denmark occurred very early in submerged site investigations and these models continue to play a pivotal role in this type of research (see Section 4). In addition to full-scale excavations, early geophysical surveys to locate inundated archaeological materials also took place. Although surveys in this period lacked adequate bathymetric maps, global positioning systems (GPS), and geographic information systems (GIS), they demonstrated the potential for using remote sensing techniques such as side-scan SONAR, sub-bottom profilers, and proton magnetometers which had been used to locate shipwrecks for locating submerged prehistoric archaeological sites. Examples include Dixon's survey in the Bering Sea (1979) and surveys to locate submerged pile dwellings in Swiss lakes (e.g., Stickel and Garrison 1988).

1.1.4 1990s–Present, Deep Prehistory

Following the demonstrated ability to conduct submerged prehistoric site discovery, excavation, and survey, the 1990s to the present have shown a dramatic growth in terms of the geographic range and time depth represented by submerged prehistoric projects. Methods have also been continuously developed to better understand these sites and their associated paleolandscapes. To date, the deepest artifact recovered is from a depth of 145 m (a retouched flake from a core in the North Sea [Long et al. 1986]) and the oldest artifacts to be found underwater are Acheulean handaxes off the coast of South Africa (Werz and Flemming 2001). These handaxes were found at a depth of 7–8 m and all three seem to be close to their in situ positions, showing little or no evidence of abrasion or other wear from traveling significant distances. These are undoubtedly the oldest archaeological materials to be recovered from submerged contexts thus far as Acheulean technology was developed and used between 300,000 and 1.4 million years ago. Therefore, the geographic and temporal scope of prehistoric archaeology available underwater covers over one million years and extends to the edge of the continental shelf, and thus, all of the once available dry land (Bailey and Flemming 2008: 2160). Our ability to explore deep time in deep depths has grown tremendously.

In addition to these early finds from South Africa, research exploring the world's continental shelves for submerged prehistoric sites has increased, including further exploration of Doggerland (e.g., Amkreutz and van der Vaart-Verschoof 2022), Sunda and Sahul (the submerged landmasses connecting southeast Asia and Australia, Tasmania, New Guinea, and the Aru Islands [Benjamin et al. 2020, 2023a, 2023b; Ditchfield et al. 2022; see also Irwanto 2019]), and both the Pacific and Atlantic continental shelves of the western hemisphere (e.g., Evans et al. 2014; Fedje and Josenhans 2000; Garrison et al. 2016; Gusick et al. 2019). In addition to these projects targeting the continental shelf, inland submerged prehistory has also grown, targeting freshwater rivers, sinkholes, cenotes, and lakes (Chatters et al. 2014; Gaspari et al. 2011; Halligan et al. 2016; Hayashida et al. 2014; O'Shea and Meadows 2009; O'Shea et al. 2014). Many of these sites will be discussed in Section 3.

This most recent time period marks a rapid increase in research projects due to continuing methods development. Advances in technology include (1) more accurate bathymetric mapping to understanding regional topography and fluctuating water levels over time, (2) the widespread use of GPS to accurately locate and map sites at sea, (3) the continued use and improvement of subsea geophysical instruments including side-scan SONAR and sub-bottom profilers to conduct archaeological survey, (4) the inclusion of AUVs to conduct archaeological surveys (the first of which was in 2000), (5) advances in coring and sediment sampling procedures, and (6) the combination of all these methods to accurately model the paleolandscape and survey for prehistoric submerged sites (see Section 4, Bailey and Flemming 2008).

One of the most significant contributions to global submerged prehistory was the SPLASHCOS – Submerged Prehistoric Archaeology and Landscapes of the Continental Shelf – initiative. Funded by the European Commission under its Cooperation in Science and Technology program, from 2009 to 2013 SPLASHCOS connected researchers conducting underwater archaeological investigations across Europe. Through a series of funded conferences and programs, archaeologists, marine geoscientists, heritage professionals, and industry partners collaborated to research and manage archaeological and paleoecological data on the European continental shelf. Thousands of archaeological sites and occurrences are displayed on the SPLASHCOS Viewer, a map of archaeological finds around Europe. Numerous significant publications emerged from SPLASHCOS (e.g., Bailey et al. 2017, 2020; Flemming et al. 2017, see also Evans et al. 2014) while connections made between researchers are still producing fruitful conversations and results, including inspiring archaeologists working in the western and southern hemispheres to create similar networks (O'Shea 2023; Ward et al. 2022).

1.1.5 Summary and Definitions

Within the four phases of the history of archaeology underwater, two primary foci of research underwater, shipwrecks and submerged sites, followed similar trajectories. There is first an early period of salvage or simply discovery of materials underwater (Phases 1 and 3), followed by a period of systematic archaeological research and methods development (Phases 2 and 4). Given the history of archaeologists working underwater, there is a vast range of sites that have been discovered and investigated, their contribution to the global archaeological record is clear, and distinct avenues of research within the broad scope of archaeology underwater can be defined:

Underwater archaeology is the systematic investigation of the human past through material remains in underwater environments.

Maritime archaeology is the investigation of the physical remains of human interactions and relationships with the sea, including ships, boats, boat-burials, abandoned hulls, sunken wrecks, and so on, and infrastructure associated with the sea including ports, harbors, docks, and lighthouses. Maritime archaeology is also interested in human behaviors on or around the water including shipping, recreation, piracy, trade, travel, warfare, folklore, ritual, etc. Maritime archaeology is therefore among the broadest terms, dealing with sites that are both terrestrial and underwater and the long (pre)history of maritime adaptations dating back to the Pleistocene, and a more anthropological understanding of maritime lifeways (see Muckelroy 1978).

Nautical archaeology as a whole fits within maritime archaeology as defined, it deals with the specialized study of ships, boats, canoes, and past floating crafts by examining their material remains. Detailed studies of fresh and saltwater vessels include standard archaeological measurements and documentation as well as historical and documentary research, iconography, ethnology, and experimental techniques. Similar to nautical archaeology and its focus on ship and wreck sites, *Aeronautical archaeology* is the study of aircraft crash sites and battlefields that are under water, within the broader field of aviation archaeology, the study of past human interaction with flight (Whitehead and Lickliter-Mundon 2023)

Submerged site archaeology is the study of any archaeological feature or site that was once land but is now completely or partially submerged. Rising water levels due to melting ice, geomorphological processes, and cataclysmic events have drowned sites that were once dry land. Sunken habitation sites, lake dwellings, or inundated cities are included as well as entire landscapes, although those are occasionally separated out into their own category of *submerged landscape studies*. *Wetland archaeology* includes sites that are waterlogged but are often investigated using different techniques than those that are completely submerged, but many of the same conservation and preservation concerns apply to both cases (see Section 5).

Submerged prehistory has a similar relationship to submerged site archaeology that nautical archaeology has with maritime archaeology, in that it is a more specialized study of specific types of sites and materials found underwater. In this case, those remains that are prehistoric, dating to time periods before preserved and/or recognized written records and other documentary sources (see Benjamin et al. 2011). Investigations of submerged prehistoric sites and landscapes often involve intensive paleoenvironmental research.

This Element will focus on these last categories of submerged sites and landscapes. Submerged sites are well within the theoretical wheelhouse of anthropology (Section 2); their formation processes are varied but they can be preserved in situ with minimal postdepositional disturbances (Section 3), methods for investigating them include well-established tactics as well as evolving technologies (Section 4), they preserve novel data with excellent organic preservation including their original paleoenvironmental contexts (Section 5), and they represent time periods that are often poorly understood or destroyed on land – contributing vital information for our understanding of the past, one that will be critical for the future (Section 6).

2 Establishing an Anthropological Archaeology Framework

How do the different categories of underwater archaeology correspond to theoretical orientations and disciplinary training? This has been slow to establish, as many of the more philosophical considerations in the field have been concerned with what is and what is not underwater archaeology, and whether it should be a distinct field of study at all. For example, many have suggested that underwater archaeology is a potentially misleading term, as at its core it is a descriptor of the environment that some archaeological sites and materials are found in, and that some archaeologists work in (Flemming 1971; Martin 2020). Numerous archaeologists (who incidentally work underwater) have stated that we do not speak of "desert" or "jungle" or "arctic" archaeology, although archaeologists overcome challenges to work in all these environments, just as they do underwater (Bass 1966; Flemming 1971; Martin 2020). But indeed, archaeologists *do* speak of desert archaeology (e.g., Alday and Morrisset 2019; Veth et al. 2005), high-altitude archaeology (e.g., Ceruti 2023), and arctic archaeology (e.g., Rowley-Conwy 1999) while we also characterize studies by periods, regions, themes, and/or techniques, for example, "Bronze Age," "South American," "Nautical," "Geoarchaeology."

It has also been stated that the fact that archaeological materials are found underwater is not directly relevant to their interpretation, although it certainly had an impact on their survival (Martin 2020). But in reality, some archaeological materials being underwater is extremely relevant to their interpretation. For example, fluctuating water levels, which have subsequently drowned and re-exposed landscapes, significantly impacted human populations in those areas. And final submergence of landscapes, particularly at the end of the Pleistocene, resulted in the loss of continental landmasses (e.g., Beringia, Doggerland, Sahul, etc.), surely the loss of these landscapes and its impact on plant, animal, and human communities is essential to the interpretation of human behavior in these places and times periods.

Arguments that underwater archaeology is simply just archaeology and that artifacts being underwater have no bearing on their interpretation largely stem from an effort to legitimize the field and stave off criticism that was leveled at underwater archaeologists and underwater materials (see Bass 1983). In order to distinguish themselves and their rigorous science from salvage or treasure hunting, underwater archaeologists sought to reassure their colleagues that they were archaeologists as well, regardless of where their data came from. Conducting archaeology underwater is a specialty, one that can be utilized just as any other in an archaeologist's toolkit, to examine material culture and investigate the past. Just as a zooarchaeologist may work on animal remains from different sites in different regions and from different time periods, an underwater archaeologist may do the same (and indeed they often do). Although their research focus is likely connected to a specific time and place or theme, their practical skills are transferable.

Underwater archaeology does require specialized methods, particularly the application of unique technologies employed in underwater science (Section 4) and the conservation of waterlogged materials (Section 5). Beyond that, however, archaeology underwater is just that – archaeology. All archaeologists look for, map, excavate sites, and analyze data. Although specialized techniques and tools have been developed to work underwater, the archaeological goals and processes are essentially the same as in any other context; conceptually, archaeology conducted underwater is no different than archaeology conducted on land (Table 1).

While conceptually archaeology is archaeology is archaeology, the study of submerged landscapes can augment, or in some cases overturn assumptions about the past based solely on terrestrial archaeology. This is largely due to the unique preservation within submerged sites, their environmental contexts, and the significant geographic areas they occupy. Coastlines around the world have been hubs of human transport, economies, and lifeways for millennia

Table 1 Archaeologies compared.

Terrestrial	Underwater
Problem definition	Problem definition
Pre-investigation research	Pre-investigation research
Site discovery	Site discovery
Site mapping	Site mapping
Data recovery	Data recovery
Analysis	Analysis
Conservation	Conservation
Breathe air	Breathe (compressed) air

(Bailey 2004), and most of these coastlines (and the archaeological evidence of these behaviors that they preserve) are now underwater. Importantly, shorelines and the associated study of the continental shelf is just *one* avenue of research for submerged sites. The study of submerged landscapes from an anthropological perspective opens a vast range of research questions and possibilities. This is a new approach as much of previous underwater investigations have focused on historical and regional questions (although see Gould 1983, 2000; Muckelroy 1978).

It is clear from the history of archaeology underwater that there are several categories of research, but there are two primary foci – wrecks and submerged sites. Coincidentally, these two foci match nearly one to one in the fields of history and anthropological archaeology, although the connection between submerged sites and anthropology has not always been clear, largely because most practitioners were trained in the British system of archaeology, and anthropologists were hostile to underwater archaeologists early on (Bass 1983: 92). This Element is an effort to make anthropology a unifying theme, and outline the state of the art methods used, which make archaeology underwater more accurate and efficient and to make it possible for non-diving archaeologists to work underwater when and as necessary (goals originally laid out by Flemming 1971: xii, but with the added emphasis on anthropology here).

Wreck sites have long been the purview of history and submerged sites the purview of archaeology, and I argue, anthropology. Differentiating underwater archaeology as history from underwater archaeology as anthropology is key. Shipwrecks have primarily been the focus of investigation, although there are very real differences within the archaeological record underwater – specifically the diversity of site types, from ship and plane wrecks to inundated cultural sites and landscapes. The discovery of such sites and their methods of development followed similar trajectories, but there are distinct points of divergence. These two types of sites are different, first in terms of the formation processes: a catastrophic event in the former, and often sea level rise in the latter. As Muckelroy acknowledges, most voyages never become part of the archaeological record (1978: 7). While only a small portion of ships become wrecks, entire landscapes and their accompanying archaeological sites have been submerged. Thus, while shipwrecks represent a single historical target, submerged sites are part of an entire landscape which can be investigated. These site types also vary in terms of archaeological visibility. Compared to historic shipwrecks and large-scale architecture known from later periods, the archaeological records of primarily foraging communities prior to 10,000 years ago, when portions of the continental shelf and inland lakes were dry land, can be ephemeral.

These differences between site types in terms of formation processes and visibility have led to different practical approaches in their investigation. First, the nature of these targets requires different survey strategies. When investigating a shipwreck the search is for a known target. Survey for submerged sites on the other hand requires a much more extensive search in which the number and character of what the sites may look like are not known a priori. In addition to the targets themselves, the scale of the survey must be much greater for submerged sites since the surrounding topography and bottom conditions are also part of the past-occupied landscape. A complete understanding of the landscape requires reconstruction of the paleoenvironment from background sediments and geomorphology and is critical for creating predictive models for where sites may be located. In contrast, for shipwreck investigations, these features are essentially incidental to discovery and largely irrelevant. Overall, the investigation of inundated cultural sites is distinct from the underwater archaeology of shipwrecks (see Benjamin et al. 2011; Lemke and O'Shea 2022; O'Shea 2021).

In order to conduct submerged site surveys and excavation then, these very real differences between shipwrecks and inundated archaeological records need to be accounted for. Ultimately, investigations of wreck sites and submerged sites have different research questions and goals and these differences stem from disciplinary roots and their associated theoretical orientations. These divergent approaches are highlighted here:

> While anthropologically oriented archaeologists continue to talk about what they plan to do next, perhaps drawing up a research design, I plan to train a number of nautical archaeologists of particularist persuasion to begin the careful examination of New World shipwrecks before the best are all destroyed by treasure hunters. (Bass 1983: 98)

> The archaeological study of shipwrecks requires approaches common to the natural, social, and historical sciences. Most shipwreck and maritime archaeological research so far has employed scientific techniques but no social-scientific hypotheses. (Gould 2000: 2)

Bass' famous plea for historical particularism and his method of training continue to be pervasive in the field. From a purely methodological standpoint, historical particularism is essential for nautical archaeology; but by design, this approach is limited in scope. With respect to Bass (1983: 96), we can take a slightly less dogmatic approach than archaeology is anthropology or it is nothing (*sensu* Willey and Phillips 1958: 2), and agree that nautical archaeology has made vast strides in building methods, documenting shipwrecks, advocating for citizen science, discouraging looting and treasure hunting, protecting wreck sites, and improving diversity and accessibility in the field (e.g., Broadwater 2023; Keith 2016; Lemke et al. 2022; McKinnon et al. 2020; O'Shea 2002; Scott-Ireton et al. 2023). However, Gould highlighted the absence of social science approaches and sought to apply a broader range of questions to the underwater archaeological record. Following Gould, a comparative, anthropological approach to the human past can allow archaeologists to work seamlessly between land and underwater, on either side of the waterline, to explore past human lifeways, particularly in the deep past and absent written records. Research designs for submerged sites must draw on the history and development of underwater archaeology in general while being continuously adapted to broader questions and earlier and more ephemeral archaeological records. These are problems that an anthropological toolkit is particularly suited for addressing. Anthropological archaeology underwater therefore combines underwater research methods, archaeological data, and anthropological theory. It builds connections between the terrestrial and underwater archaeological records to create a holistic picture of past landscapes and human communities therein (Lemke 2016).

What larger questions about human behavior can submerged sites and landscapes address? How can research be designed, and data applied to ask and answer anthropological research questions? See Lemke for areas where submerged sites can contribute to questions such as early human evolution and the origins of human culture, global human expansion, maritime adaptations, and early seafaring (2021). Here two topics – human responses to climate change and the antiquity of hunter-gatherer complexity – will be briefly discussed to highlight the engaged bodies of theory within anthropological studies to which underwater data can be applied.

Given the dramatic rise in sea level at the end of the last ice age and the vast amount of habitable land that was submerged, it is no surprise that many studies of drowned prehistoric landscapes can address climate change. For example, the discovery of many Mesolithic sites in the Baltic reflects dramatic sea level rise, giving archaeologists a unique case study for understanding human decision-making during water level changes. Some Mesolithic foraging societies needed to adapt to new areas and environments while old hunting grounds were being flooded over the course of individual lifetimes (Fischer 1995a). Was sea level rise and climatic variation responsible for social changes seen in the archaeological record in the Mesolithic (Astrup 2018)? The rate and nature of rising water levels were not uniform across Scandinavia and while some areas experienced dramatic changes, others did not. This provides an ideal laboratory for studying human responses to environmental change with a comparative approach. Were social changes uniform across the region, or not? What, if any, social changes did occur, when, and how? Willerslev has shown that while often assumed, hunter-gatherer communities do not always change in response to environmental fluctuations (2009). Cultural adaptations and climate change are incredibly relevant topics in our contemporary world (Gaffney 2022) and contrasting responses to anthropogenic climate change to cultural responses to past environmental change would be an interesting approach. Along those lines, engagement with the concept of resilience in anthropology (Eitel 2023; Wakefield et al. 2020) can be applied to archaeological data from submerged sites. Many past populations were living on the "front lines" of climate change and were resilient in their behavior, as shown by the 7,000-year-old seawall discovered underwater in Israel (Galili et al. 2019).

Submerged landscapes have revealed patterns of settlement, subsistence, and lifeways that are unknown on land (Bailey and Flemming 2008: 2162). For example, submerged Mesolithic sites off the Danish coast are large settlements, which reveal a more socially complex culture than evidence from archaeological sites on land seemed to indicate (e.g., Andersen 2013; Fischer 1995b). Tybrind Vig and other submerged Mesolithic sites reveal that peoples in this time were more complex and dynamic than traditionally hypothesized based on terrestrial data alone. These studies can be applied to a discussion of social complexity more broadly and the nature of hunter-gatherers (e.g., Grier et al. 2006; Thompson 2022). Additionally, investments in the built landscape by hunter-gatherers have not been widely recognized, particularly dating to the late Pleistocene/early Holocene; but submerged landscape studies in the North American Great Lakes have documented some of the world's oldest hunting architecture, stone-constructed features including hunting blinds and drive lanes (Lemke 2022; O'Shea and Meadows 2009; O'Shea et al. 2014). Such structures are an example of niche construction and are the physical remains of traditional ecological knowledge (Lemke 2021b, 2022). While adding unique data points to the record, neither of these cases should be surprising as without the submerged record, only part of the story was known – again revealing how critical submerged landscapes were for the people once living upon them, and certainly for archaeologists studying these time periods. With the large array of archaeological site types preserved below water, and the theoretical perspective to factor their data into broader questions about human behavior, underwater archaeologists are in a unique position to directly contribute to theory.

3 Types of Sites: Our Cultural World, Submerged

The underwater archaeological record is vast and varied. While most conceptions of underwater archaeology focus solely on shipwrecks, the range of site types found below water is the same as that on land. In fact, wreck sites are the outlier in archaeology – where planes or vessels have sunk and/or crashed – creating a unique historical time capsule, but one that is accidental. There, the surrounding context makes little difference and, rather than an aggregate of human behavior over time, these sites represent a snapshot (see Section 3.2 and Lemke and O'Shea 2022). In contrast, submerged sites exist on a spectrum, from Pompeii-like to palimpsests. For the former, sites like Port Royal, which drowned after an earthquake in 1692 (Hamilton 1984, see Section 3.4.2), are a snapshot of formal and spatial relationships that are characteristic of one specific moment in time. In contrast, other archaeological sites have accumulated over the use life of the site or region and are palimpsests of formal and spatial relationships. They represent repeated behavior over time, such as the ritual deposits in Chichén Itzá. Just as on land, archaeological sites underwater are diverse and unique, subject to a range of formation processes and pre- and postdepositional transformations (Lemke and O'Shea 2022). These range from geological to cultural and affect the spatial distribution, preservation, and deposition of archaeological materials. Some formation processes are unique to underwater environments, such as the initial submergence of these areas, wave action, hurricanes, subsidence, currents, and disturbance by marine animals such as lobsters burrowing into cultural layers, Figure 1. Disturbance may also include scour marks, anchor drags, and dredging operations, (although the latter activity has also been responsible for the discovery of many submerged sites, see Section 4). However, despite these postdepositional impacts, compared to many places on land the disturbance from subsequent construction and human habitation has been much less, particularly when sites are far offshore and in deep water, and thus less accessible. Despite assumptions that wave action and flooding would leave underwater deposits hopelessly mixed or

Figure 1 A lobster burrows into cultural layers at Bouldnor Cliff, a prehistoric
settlement site in the Solent, United Kingdom. Photograph courtesy
of Garry Momber.

disturbed, submerged sites preserve detailed and intact stratigraphy, such as at
the Page-Ladson site in Florida (Halligan et al. 2016).

Since these sites and landscapes are relatively well protected, there are time
periods that may be unknown or deeply buried on land which are preserved
underwater. For example, in the North American Great Lakes, archaeological
sites dating to the late Pleistocene/early Holocene are poorly known from the
terrestrial record due to acidic soils, isostatic rebound/glacial uplift, dune
formation, and water level regression (Lemke 2015; Lovis et al. 2012).
However, 9,000-year-old sites and associated artifacts are preserved underwater
on a submerged landform that was once dryland in Lake Huron (O'Shea and
Meadows 2009; O'Shea et al. 2014, see below). The deep water (35 m) and
offshore location (80 km) of these submerged sites have preserved this unique
evidence. Significantly, underwater landscapes preserve not just archaeological
materials but background sediments, topography, and environmental indicators,
which reflect the past-occupied landscape. Paleoenvironments can be reconstructed from preserved pollen, trees, and other organic remains to put archaeological sites in their broader environmental, climatic, and ecological context
while also aiding models of site prediction (see Section 4).

Overall, the various site types preserved underwater supplement each other,
and their unique preservation makes them a particularly valuable complement

to the terrestrial record and a vital part of world archaeology. Here the types of non-wreck, submerged sites are organized into four categories of formation processes: intentional deposits, catastrophic sites, the remains of lake dwellings, and marine transgression/regression deposits, that is, those drowned by fluctuating water levels. It should also be noted that there are some recorded incidences of loss in the underwater record, distinct from these categories. Examples include broken pieces of water jars recovered from the Xlacah cenote at Dzibilchaltún, Yucatán (Andrews 1959; Marden 1959) and broken amphorae dating to numerous periods between the second and seventh centuries found in a submerged cave in the south of France (Billaud 2017). All of these are likely the remains of vessels breaking against the rock wall and/or falling in when individuals were gathering water and represent incidental loss rather than other types of deposits.

3.1 Intentional Deposits

Rather than accidental deposits or loss, there are a number of examples of intentionality in the submerged record, including refuse sites, ritual deposits, votive offerings, and burials. Obviously, the first of these, refuse sites, is significantly different from the other examples of intentional deposits. Some submerged archaeological materials appear to be underwater middens, where populations living near water would dispose of their trash within it. Evidence for refuse sites comes from Florida, including Oven Hill, an eighteenth-century Seminole site on the bank of the Suwannee River where many broken pieces of pottery have been recovered just offshore, and Fig Springs, where several thousand artifacts from different time periods have been recovered from the Ichtucknee River and interpreted as a refuse pile (Goggin 1960). The Ryan-Harley site in the Wacissa River is the only known Middle Paleoindian midden in the region (Dunbar et al. 2006; Smith 2020).

In stark contrast to refuse, ritual use and deposits in bodies of water are still common throughout the world and were common in the past as well (e.g., Billaud 2017; Campbell 2017; Kinkella and Lucero 2017: 198). Outlining the long (pre)history of these practices is another line of inquiry that would make an informative anthropological study. Specific examples include Mayan artifacts recovered from the cenote at Chichén Itzá, including the obsidian, gold, and jadeite figurines mentioned above but also shell, wood, rubber, and cloth artifacts. Mayan incense burners and other artifacts in Lakes Amatitlán and Petén Itzá, Guatemala (Andrews and Corletta 1995; Borhegyi 1958, 1959), and Mayan ceramics in Actun Ek Nen at the Cara Blanca Pools, Belize (Kinkella and Lucero 2017) are further evidence of ritual deposits. Underwater ritual caches are found at many sites in the Maya area, including the Cenote Azul in Chipas (Andrews and Corletta 1995: 107). The pre-Hispanic objects, including ceramic vessels and a jade axe, recovered from a cenote on Cozumel are also interpreted as offerings (Luna Erreguerena 1989: 150). Inca offerings in Lake Titicaca include over two dozen stone boxes with human and llama figurines made out of silver, gold, and *Spondylus* shell, as well as miniature gold ornaments which were intentionally submerged on an underwater reef (Delaere and Capriles 2020). In the Dominican Republic, research in the limestone-flooded sinkhole of Manantial de la Aleta revealed that it was used as an offering site by the Taíno people. Wood, basketry, gourds, feathered regalia, and a *macana* (war club) are preserved in an archaeological deposit 35 m underwater (Conrad et al. 2005; Maus et al. 2017). There is a sulfur layer between 5–10 m so offerings deposited into the sinkhole would have been seen disappearing into the underworld (John Foster personal communication 2023). Votive offerings are common throughout history in the Thames River, including an extensive collection of metalwork (Lawrence 1929; York 2002). In addition to metal, other materials including stone, ceramic, and human remains have been recovered during dredging operations in the river, including the Battersea Shield, thought to be an offering (Bradley and Gordon 1988; Lawrence 1929; Stead 1985). Indeed, deliberate deposits into rivers in the Late Bronze Age are a well-documented phenomenon in northwest Europe, particularly in larger rivers such as the Thames and Seine (Jasinski and Warmenbol 2017: 166). In Belgium, Trou de Han in Hans-sur-Lesse is a cave and river system where an impressive array of archaeological materials has been recovered. There is evidence of ritual deposits into the river from the Late Neolithic to the Roman period, including some objects that were intentionally broken or "ritually killed" before being deposited into the water and others that are intact. They range in material and artifact type including bone/antler, bronze, and gold spearheads, horse-bits, ornaments, axes, and spoons. Many of the objects found underwater in the river are the same type of objects that are found in burials during these various periods (Delaere and Warmenbol 2019; Jasinski and Warmenbol 2017). In North America, colonoware bowls engraved with an "X" mark have been found discarded in water, such as rivers near plantations. These have been interpreted to relate to Bakongo cosmology and were ritually deposited in bodies of water by enslaved peoples (Ferguson 1992: 110–117).

Burials are among the most intentional deposits to be encountered by archaeologists and some were specifically placed in water. The water mortuary cult of the southeastern United States provides the best example of intentional deposits in watery graves, as individuals were wrapped in textiles, bundled, and then placed in peat bog environments. Wooden stake remains are interpreted as holding bodies down while the top part of the stakes may have served as markers above the water level. Windover (Florida) is the best known of these sites, with outstanding organic preservation of textiles, wooden artifacts, and human remains dating between 5000–6000 cal yr BP (Doran 2002). Other sites also have underwater burials in peat in Florida including Little Salt Spring, Bay West, and Republic Grove (e.g., Clausen et al. 1979; see also Gifford et al. 2017). Most recently another cemetery in this tradition was located in the Gulf of Mexico. While offshore now, Manasota Key was once a swampy freshwater peat bog surrounded by dry land, where bodies were intentionally placed (Duggins et al. 2018; Smith et al. 2022). Manasota Key is an interesting case study of intentional deposits into a wetland that is now entirely submerged in saltwater given water level transgression. Numerous other burials and human remains have been discovered at submerged sites, but in those cases, the burials were originally on land and then drowned by sea level rise (e.g., Tybrind Vig [see section 1.1.3], Warm Mineral Springs, Florida [Lenihan et al. 2017], and Atlit-Yam [see section 3.4.1]).

3.2 Catastrophic Deposits

There are a number of cities that are submerged due to catastrophic events. Catastrophic sites exist on both land and underwater, including places such as Pompeii and Herculaneum in Italy, the Ozette site in the United States, and Port Royal in Jamaica (Hamilton 2006). These sites were created by some disaster that preserved archaeological materials and their context. Ozette was covered over by a landslide, while Pompeii and Herculaneum were covered in ash, and Port Royal as well as Minoan and Mycenean port cities and others were submerged as the result of tectonic activity. On June 7, 1692, an earthquake struck Port Royal and submerged two-thirds of the town in a matter of minutes (Hamilton 1984, 2006). While portions of the city were extensively damaged from the earthquake and sinking, other areas are preserved nearly intact, and systematic long-term archaeological research at the site provides a detailed view of one of the largest late seventeenth-century English colonial port cities in the Americas (Hamilton 1984).

In 1968, Nic Flemming discovered inundated structures including walls and rock-cut tombs in shallow water at Pavlopetri near the southern tip of mainland Greece. Starting in 2007, systematic research has been conducted on this submerged urban site. Nearly a complete town has been mapped using both conventional and digital methods covering over 9,000 m^2. First thought to date to the early Mycenaean period, ceramic artifacts extend the occupation back to the Minoan Bronze Age, 4800 years ago, making this the world's oldest submerged city. A true example of maritime archaeology, Pavlopetri also has a harbor, and it may be linked to the rich archaeological record underwater of shipwrecks in the Mediterranean (Flemming 1971; Harding et al. 1969; Mahon et al. 2011). Apollonia, on Libya's northeast or Cyrenaic coast, was an important harbor in the southern Mediterranean and now much of the site is 2–2.5 m underwater, due to earthquakes/subsidence (Flemming 1980, 2021). Around Greece in the Saronic Gulf, coastlines have changed significantly over the past 5,000 years in the tectonically active Aegean and a series of submerged or partially submerged Bronze Age harbors have been discovered. Underwater surveys at Kalamianos, for example, reported ceramics and wood charcoal (Pullen 2013). The archaeological site of Baiae, Italy, is partially submerged in the Mediterranean due to volcanic activity, and roads, statues, and mosaics of this Roman town are preserved in shallow water just offshore from the rest of the site (Bruno et al. 2015).

A combination of seismic activity and rising sea levels sunk the Egyptian port city of Thonis-Heracleion. Numerous expeditions to the site have recovered and mapped statuary, pottery, coins, etc. within and around the remains of temples and other structures. Given the location of this port city and the discovery of shipwrecks near the site, this is another example of maritime archaeology (Robinson and Goddio 2015). Also in Egypt is Cleopatra's Palace or Antirhodos, once an island in the eastern harbor of Alexandria until earthquakes and tsunamis sank the remains of a Ptolemaic palace. Indeed, numerous architectural remains from different sites have been found in the eastern harbor of Alexandria (El-Rayis et al. 2003; Khalil and Mustafa 2002). Tectonic activity on the Matano Fault Zone in Matano Lake, Indonesia submerged at least five archaeological sites, with remains including iron tools, iron slag, ceramics, and wooden poles (Dhony et al. 2023). Catastrophic deposits such as these submerged cities are most similar to shipwrecks in that their formation happened quickly, sometimes within minutes such as Port Royal, and thus they preserve unique snapshots of everyday life and materials.

3.3 Lake Dwelling Deposits

A range of sites represent portions of lake dwellings, including pile dwellings and artificial islands made on the shores of lakes, as well as rivers and wetlands, which became inundated in many parts of the world. The best-known examples include the remains of over 1000 pile dwellings, or stilt houses, in the Alpine regions of France, Switzerland, Germany, Austria, Italy, and Slovenia. These archaeological sites were designated as World Heritage Sites and are some of those that were originally seen on early aerial maps. Built on marshy land, such dwellings were raised to protect against occasional flooding. Now, as water levels have fluctuated over time, many of the original piles or stilts are preserved below water. Neolithic pile dwellings have also been discovered and excavated in shallow water lakes in Northwest Russia (Mazurkevich and Dolbunova 2011) and a 6,000-year-old pile dwelling, Zambratija, has been investigated under the Adriatic Sea (Jerbic 2020).

In Scotland, crannogs are partially or entirely artificially constructed islands with settlements, usually with a bridge or causeway joining them to shore. Similar to the lake dwellings, these sites have a wide range of organic materials and environmental evidence preserved underwater, some dating to the early Iron Age (Dixon 2004). Underwater excavations at the Ederline Crannog encountered structural timbers and animal bones (Cavers and Henderson 2005). Similarly, the Mayan island of Jaina is partially artificial, and water levels have submerged a large portion of its western edge (Andrews and Corletta 1995; Piña Chan 1968: 27–28).

3.4 Marine Transgression/Regression Deposits

Most submerged sites are the result of water level fluctuations that inundated past cultural landscapes, those that have resulted from marine transgression or transgression/regression cycles. Marine transgression and regression are complicated, multivariate geological processes involving global water budgets, relative humidity/aridity, erosion and channel features, glaciation, precipitation, and isostatic rebound. The last two million years during which sea levels fluctuated and drowned much of the world's continental shelves correspond to a long period in human prehistory during which many significant changes occurred. This time period in fact encapsulates the entire trajectory from the origins of modern humans and their migration across the planet to the development of agriculture. Particularly relevant for archaeologists is the marine regression that happened during glaciation and the global rise in water levels at the end of the last ice age. At the end of the Pleistocene, global sea level rose 120–130 m as the ice sheets retreated (Lambeck et al. 2002; Lisiecki and Raymo 2005). After this significant rise, water levels continued to fluctuate throughout the Holocene, though to a lesser extent.

The areas of land which were exposed prior to global sea level rise were extremely vast. The Patagonian region in Argentina, for example, was almost double its present size (Guilderson et al. 2000). Understandably, given the geographic spread and topographic and environmental variation in these landscapes, there is no single method that has proved useful for submerged landscapes studies all over the world. Instead, archaeologists have employed a range of multidisciplinary and layered techniques (Section 4). Important lessons have been learned including that water level fluctuations and sea level curves vary widely on local and regional scales and models for one part of the world cannot be adopted for another. Even on a small scale, water level fluctuations are not uniform nor systematic. Furthermore, while lower water levels affected the entire planet, there are significant differences between the northern and southern hemispheres in modeling water levels, as the northern hemisphere was also subject to isostatic rebound and glacial pulses. While understanding glacial boundaries is a well-known geological problem as glacializations effectively erase evidence of prior glacial extents, isostatic rebound is similarly complicated as former lake shores and beach ridges can be elevated high above contemporary shorelines, while across the same lake basin, other shorelines will be deeply buried or submerged.

Despite these challenges for investigators, submerged landscapes would have been some of the most valuable areas on the landscape for hunting, gathering, fishing, and early farming societies. When dry land, these areas would have been very attractive as coastlines are productive ecotones between the sea and land where a wide variety of resources are available. These areas therefore probably housed some of the highest population densities, making them crucial landscapes for the spread of people and ideas between different regions, and ultimately around the globe (e.g., Bailey 2011; Fischer 1995a; Flemming 2004, 2011; Johnson and Stright 1992; Masters and Flemming 1983; Westley et al. 2011). Because of this archaeological potential, and the sheer size of land on the world's continental shelves that was lost to marine transgression, much of the work by submerged prehistorians has focused on these areas (see Bailey et al. 2017, 2020; Evans et al. 2014; Flemming et al. 2017). Some of these projects are highlighted below.

3.4.1 Continental Shelves

Doggerland is roughly 23,000 km^2 now submerged beneath the North Sea, but was once a terrestrial landscape of hills, rivers, swamps, and shorelines (Martin 2020) demonstrated by finds including plants, animal bones, human remains, and artifacts. While there are many artifacts that have washed up on beaches around the North Sea, long-term research projects in the nearshore in the Solent and the Baltic have produced striking results. Bouldnor Cliff in the United Kingdom, in the western Solent near Southampton is the site of an eroding cliff 11 m beneath the surface which has preserved and revealed a buried archaeological landscape dating to around 8000 years ago. Mesolithic materials including worked wood, stone tools, food remains, plant fibers, hearths, preserved peat, and a wooden platform have been recovered (Figures 2a–b).

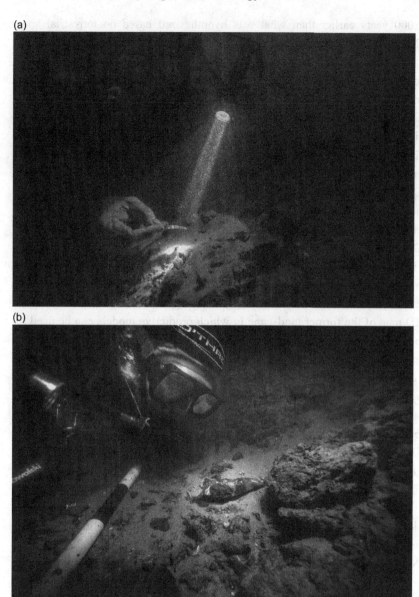

Figure 2 (a) A diver inspects and records Mesolithic lithic artifacts eroding from submerged landscape strata at Bouldnor Cliff, a prehistoric settlement site in the Solent, United Kingdom **(b)** diver closely inspects a lithic artifact and debitage. Photographs courtesy of Garry Momber.

The archaeological evidence at Bouldnor Cliff, aided by the unique preservation of organics underwater, reveals that the technological aspects of Mesolithic peoples were far more refined, and the technical competence is

2,000 years earlier than what was hypothesized based on terrestrial sites (Momber 2000; Momber et al. 2011).

On the eastern extent of Doggerland, off the southern portion of Funen Island in Denmark, a range of Mesolithic Erebølle sites have been discovered and investigated (Astrup 2018). As mentioned above, these demonstrate unique aspects of forager life in the Mesolithic and document community response to rising water levels. Additional research in and around Doggerland has recorded finds made by the public as well as archaeological investigations and paleo-environmental reconstructions (Amkreutz and van der Vaart-Verschoof 2022). On the nearshore at Happisburgh in the United Kingdom, early Pleistocene hominin footprints have been recorded, revealed by coastal erosion (Ashton et al. 2014). In addition to Fermanville (see Section 1), Bouldnor Cliff, and the Danish sites, in situ archaeological remains were encountered in Yangtze Harbour in the Netherlands revealing Mesolithic tools and food residues from hunter-gatherer occupations before the landscape was drowned (Schiltmans 2022). Research further offshore and into Doggerland has provided a detailed 3D map of the former landscape in which predictive models can be used to better understand the topography and human use of these areas (Gaffney et al. 2009; Gaffney and Fitch 2022). However, much of Doggerland still remains *terra* (or rather *aqua*) *incognita*, no confirmed archaeological settlement or in situ evidence has been recovered beyond the nearshore or in depths greater than 20 m (Gaffney 2022: 8). However, the presence of preserved environmental remains and chance finds at greater depths in Doggerland, including a Neanderthal brow ridge 15 km from shore (Hublin et al. 2009), provide further evidence of the dry land environment and archaeological potential.

Apart from Doggerland, numerous other submerged sites have been documented on the world's continental shelves. These include Neolithic settlements on the Carmel Coast of Israel such as Atlit-Yam, a Pre-Pottery Neolithic habitation site in 8–12 m of water. The site is one of the earliest to provide evidence of maritime activity and has excellent preservation of floral and faunal remains, as well as lithic tools, architecture, and human burials (Galili et al. 1993). There are also other sites found in this region, including later-aged, submerged settlements from the Pottery Neolithic. Together, along with paleoenvironmental data, these sites reveal that the Mediterranean remained ~30 m lower than present into the early Holocene. Coastal occupation could therefore continue until rising waters eventually submerged these areas (Galili et al. 1993). Evidence of human responses to sea level rise includes the 7,000-year-old now-submerged sea wall (Section 2), the oldest coastal defense in the world (Galili et al. 2019).

On Australia's continental shelf, the search for submerged sites is critical as two million km^2 of land would have been available during the last glacial period (Benjamin et al. 2020). Intertidal zones have produced evidence of quarries, artifacts, and fish traps (e.g., Rowland and Ulm 2011). On the continental shelf itself, artifacts have been reported from the Murujuga coastline and Dampier Archipelago in Northwestern Australia (Figure 3, Benjamin et al. 2020, 2023; Dortch et al. 2019; Wiseman et al. 2021).

In the western hemisphere, on the Atlantic continental shelf, surveys and excavations have taken place in the Gulf of Mexico with sub-bottom profilers, side-scan SONAR, and coring to locate sites dating the Paleoindian and Archaic periods (e.g., Adovasio and Hemmings 2009). Many have been located and excavated, primarily off the coast of Florida such as the J&J Hunt site, by Faught (2004). Faught and Smith provide a summary of submerged prehistoric sites found by systematic geoarchaeological approaches on continental shelves in the western hemisphere (2021), including evidence of an intertidal midden, lithic quarries, and a preserved Maya wooden paddle from Belize (McKillop 2005). On the Pacific coast continental shelf, projects include Haida Gwaii, Canada (Fedje et al. 2004; Fedje and Josenhans 2000; Josenhans et al. 1995, 1997) where a lithic artifact was recovered from 53 m of water and dates to an estimated 10,000 years ago and a potential fishing weir located in Shakan Bay,

Figure 3 Underwater artifact (A10) found in the Cape Bruguieres Channel by divers working on the Deep History of Sea Country Project. Photo courtesy of Jonathan Benjamin (after Wisemen et al. 2021).

Alaska (Figures 4a–b, Monteleone et al. 2021). Further south in Chile, numerous extinct faunal remains have been recovered, which may show signs of human-made cutmarks at the site GNL Quintero 1 (Carabias et al. 2014). The coastal site of La Olla off of Argentina is an Early-Middle Holocene occupation (7,400–6,480 cal yr BP) (Bayón and Politis 2014). La Olla has intact deposits and exceptional preservation of organic remains, which include animal bones, plant materials, and wooden technology. It has been investigated four separate times when local tides have been abnormally low and the site was exposed. Due to the brief interval of exposure, no large-scale excavations were done. Instead, rescue operations consisted of mapping artifacts in three dimensions and the collection of sediment samples for paleoenvironmental analysis and chronometric dating (Bayón and Politis 2014). Isolated finds from submerged contexts have also been found in the area, such as a wooden fishhook recovered from the North Patagonian Coast (Gómez Otero 2007).

When examining the continental shelves for archaeological sites, most have sought or expected to recover evidence of past coastal occupations dating to time periods of lower water levels. Shell middens are common archaeological indicators of coastal settlement and marine resource extraction, but they were relatively rare across the globe before the mid-Holocene, of course likely due to sea level rise. As indicators of coastal activities, early shell middens would now be submerged. Four intact, culturally created shell middens underwater have been recorded and investigated, a Mesolithic shell midden offshore of Denmark, a Late Archaic shell midden in the Gulf of Mexico (Astrup et al. 2019; Cook Hale et al. 2021), a 7,000-year-old shell midden in Montague Harbour, British Columbia, and a Jomon period shell midden in Japan. The Hjarnø midden in the Straits of Denmark has anthropogenically burnt shells as well as stone, bone, and wooden artifacts at a depth of 0.4–1.4 m. The Middle to Late Archaic midden in the Ecofina Channel in the Gulf of Mexico in 2–4 m has a preserved shell as well as stone artifacts (Faught and Donoghue 1997). The Montague Harbour project recovered evidence of intertidal and marine shell midden deposits, including lithic debitage and debris (Easton et al. 2021). The Awazu Site is a shell midden resting in 2–3 m of water in Lake Biwa, Japan's largest freshwater lake. Awazu has cultural debris dating to the Initial and Middle Jomon Periods, 9,300 and 4,500 cal yr BP, respectively (Iba 2005; Nakagawa 2014). Importantly, intact shell middens represent a good target for underwater research as they have specific sedimentological profiles that can be identified in core samples.

3.4.2 Inland Lakes, Rivers, Sinkholes, Cenotes, and Caves

Global processes of water level fluctuations on the continental shelves are mirrored at regional levels in inland lakes, rivers, sinkholes, caves, and cenotes.

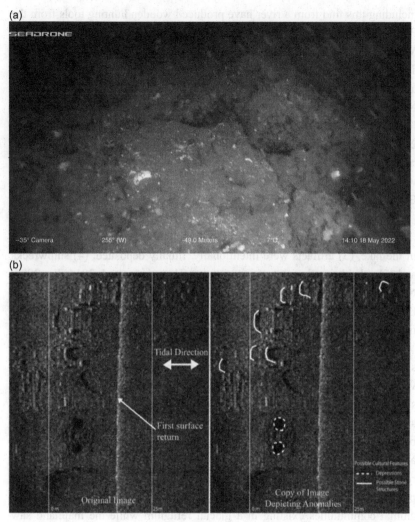

Figure 4 (a) Fishing weir, Shikáan Óot'l, from SeaDrone ROV. NOAA 2022
OER: Our Submerged Past: Exploring Inundated Late Pleistocene Caves in
Southeast Alaska with Sunfish, Shakan Bay, northwest side of Prince of Wales
Island, USA. Photograph courtesy of Kelly Monteleone. **(b)** SONAR image of
raised semicircular features and two depressions, Shakan Bay, northwest side of
Prince of Wales Island, USA. Raw SONAR image (left), image with anomalies
depicted in white (right). Image courtesy of Kelly Monteleone (after
Monteleone 2013).

The earliest artifact known from an inland underwater site is a wooden point
recovered from the Ljubljanica River in Slovenia which was radiocarbon dated
between 43,970 and 38,490 ± 330 cal yr BP. Only five archaeological sites

including this find from a river have produced wooden hunting tools from the Paleolithic (the others are Clacton-on-Sea, Lehringen, Schöningen, and Mannheim) (Gaspari et al. 2011). Although the wooden point was not in situ and seems to have eroded from older sediments into the river, the anaerobic underwater environment preserved this rare organic artifact. Submerged Neolithic sites have been excavated in lakes including a late Neolithic fishing fence, which was preserved in Lake Arendsee, Germany (Leineweber et al. 2011). Underwater research in Walker Lake in Nevada has revealed intact, buried terrestrial landforms below the lake dating from time periods of lower water levels (Puckett 2021). There are over ninety archaeological sites in Lake Biwa, Japan. There are several hypotheses to explain their presence including (1) terrestrial sites which were washed out into the lake by a rise in water level, (2) pottery and other artifacts from facilities on the shoreline were thrown away in the lake, (3) artifacts were intentionally, ritually deposited, (4) shipwrecks and (5) subsidence due to tectonic activity (Hayashida et al. 2014; Iba 2005; Nakagawa 2014). More research on the formation processes of sites in Lake Biwa will likely support many of these hypotheses as materials from various time periods have been recovered at different depths within the lake.

Water levels in the North American Great Lakes saw periods of both regression and transgression and reconstructions are complicated by glacial readvances and retreats as well as isostatic rebound, where the land is still rising slowly from the removed weight of Pleistocene glaciers. One period produced significantly lower water levels, known as Lake Stanley in the Lake Huron basin. A unique geological feature, the Alpena-Amberley Ridge (AAR) is a limestone and dolomite outcrop that resisted glacial erosion and currently rests at an average of 25 m below water. The AAR acted as a causeway for prehistoric animal migrations in the early Holocene and had unique plant and animal communities existing in a glacial refugium while the mainland saw warmer climates. The AAR also served as the locus for foragers in the region who used large glacial cobbles and boulders to construct hunting architecture features to target animals during migrations (Lemke 2022). Over sixty stone-built constructions have been discovered below Lake Huron and three of these are large, complex structures that have seen intensive archaeological excavation and sample recovery, generating organic remains of plants, trees, and lithic artifacts, including two obsidian flakes that sourced to a geological deposit over 4,000 km away (Figures 5–6, O'Shea et al. 2021).

Inundated prehistoric sites are common in the karstic sinkholes of inland Florida where Pleistocene fossils and archaeological materials have been recovered by avocational SCUBA divers and archaeologists for over fifty years (see Section 1, Smith 2022; Smith et al. 2022). Indeed, karstic sinkholes

Figure 5 Diver mapping a 9,000-year-old stone constructed feature on the Alpena-Amberley Ridge, Lake Huron, Great Lakes, USA.

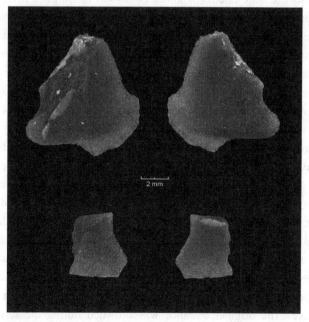

Figure 6 Obsidian artifacts recovered from South Gap, a submerged archaeological site on the Alpena-Amberley Ridge, Lake Huron, Great Lakes, USA.

and rivers on the Florida peninsula as well as the continental shelf along its coast have produced more recorded inundated prehistoric sites and artifacts than any other state in the United States, the majority of which are late Pleistocene-early Holocene in age (Clausen et al. 1975, 1979; Dunbar 1991; Faught 2004; Webb 2006). These sites provide classes of data, such as bone and ivory rods, human soft tissue, and carved and modified wood that are extremely limited in the terrestrial record (Clausen et al. 1979). Page-Ladson in Florida has preserved human artifacts and associated megafaunal remains from 14,500 years ago (Halligan et al. 2016) and is one of the oldest sites in the western hemisphere.

Similar to the karstic landscape of Florida, research in cenotes in México, specifically in the state of Quintana Roo, has produced striking results. Long-term investigations have recovered artifacts, animal bones, and human remains. In Hoyo Negro, numerous paleontological specimens have been recovered and paleobotanical remains recovered from submerged bat guano both reveal a complex picture of the paleoenvironment. While human remains dating to the Maya period have been known from cenotes, the much older remains of a woman, Naia, in Hoyo Negro date between 12,900 and 12,700 years ago (Chatters et al. 2014). At the time of Naia's death, most of the cave would have been dry and it is hypothesized she died by falling into Hoyo Negro, a similar hypothesis for the large amount of animal bones surrounding her. Investigations in now-submerged caves across the Yucatán continue to reveal evidence of late Pleistocene-early Holocene human use. Naia and other skeletal remains suggest individuals died within the caves (rather than being deposited there later); but why people were exploring the caves is an open question. One hypothesis is that individuals were entering the then-dry cave system to mine for ochre, as evidence of ochre extraction pits, cairns, and hearths has been documented (Figures 7a–b, MacDonald et al. 2020).

There are numerous sites similar to Hoyo Negro that are/were either sink-holes or caves, that become flooded, (or saw rising water levels), through water transgression events. For example, Cueva de Padre Nuestro is a cavern in the Dominican Republic that likely flooded ~6,500 years ago when worldwide sea levels rose to within 3 m of modern day (Maus et al. 2017: 205). While some submerged caves in the Dominican Republic have evidence of ritual behavior, such as Manantial de la Aleta (see section 3.1), others including Cueva de Padre Nuestro have archaeological evidence of utilitarian use for drinking and cook-ing activities (Maus et al. 2017). Cosquer Cave in France is another partially flooded cave. The original entrance was drowned during the last ice age transgression, but interior parts of the cave have remained dry and preserve Paleolithic cave paintings. Charcoal from one of the horse paintings was dated

Figure 7 A SCUBA diver **(a)** measures and **(b)** records cairn markers
in submerged caves in Yucatán Peninsula, Quintana Roo, México.
Photographs courtesy of El Centro Investigador del Sistema Acuífero de
Quintana Roo A.C. (CINDAQ).

to 18,000 cal yr BP and evidence of use dates to both Gravettian and Solutrean
periods (Clottes et al. 2017).

Canoes have been recovered from several lakes. Examples include Lake
Kenner in Missouri (Campbell 2017) and Lake Mendota in Wisconsin (Zant
et al. 2023). Many have been found in Florida (Figure 8). Over thirty years ago,
Bass appropriately questioned why so much attention was given to the "urban
revolution" rather than a "seafaring revolution," particularly given that early

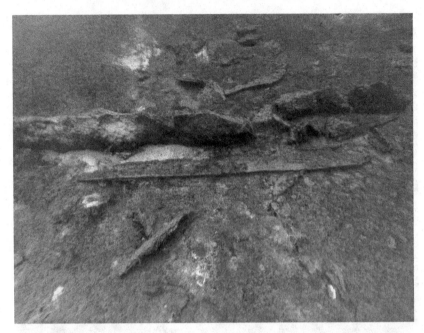

Figure 8 Remnants of a protohistoric dugout canoe in Lovers Leap Spring, central Florida, USA. Photograph courtesy of Morgan F. Smith.

seafaring and river travel predate the emergence of agriculture, metallurgy, and urbanization and that these nautical technological advances would have played a significant role in the movement of goods, people, and ideas for thousands of years (1983:92). Indirect evidence of canoes has also been recovered, such as a cache of jade artifacts off the coast of Cozumel that may be the cargo of a Maya trading canoe (Leshikar 1988: 22) and the Mayan wooden paddle (McKillip 2005). In Bass' words, there were sailors before there were farmers, and submerged site archaeology will hopefully address these important cultural developments aided by the preservation of canoes and other materials correlated with life in/on/at the water.

Finally, there are many sites that were once terrestrial that have been drowned in the last century due to large-scale dam and reservoir construction. Not caused by natural marine transgression or regression events, rather there are terrestrial sites which were flooded by human-made constructions. In ideal cases, these areas were subject to cultural resource survey before being submerged (e.g., Perttula et al. 1966). These flooded areas cover large swaths of land and different site types from a range of time periods, including cemeteries and entire towns. A unique category of submerged sites, these areas would be ideal locations for equipment testing and methods development, particularly for submerged site surveys. In locations with cultural resource management reports, site locations are known and could be revisited using techniques outlined in Section 4 to further test their voracity. Repeated, systematic monitoring of such sites would also provide data concerning the degradation (or preservation) of different material classes and record postdepositional processes over time. Effectively creating something akin to an experimental record. These are fruitful areas of future research.

There is a striking array of site types preserved below water aside from wrecks. While more sites are being discovered every year, each represents a unique contribution to the archaeological record – contributions that go beyond cultural historical data points and can be factored into broader questions about human history and behavior. Critically, the most successful submerged site research has been the result of sustained, long-term projects, with interdisciplinary, collaborative teams and layered methods.

4 Methods

One of the most distinguishing features of archaeology underwater is its methods. While terrestrial archaeology has its own suite of techniques, some more complex than others, underwater archaeology uses most of these while also incorporating the necessary technologies for working in an underwater environment. While many of the original approaches used by underwater archaeologists were developed for the discovery and investigation of shipwrecks, methods can be tailored to the research question. For example, during shipwreck excavation, the seafloor (or lakebed) that the vessel is resting on is noted but is often not consequential to the wreck. Except for incidences of grounding, the bottom has nothing to do with the site – the vessel just happened to sink there. In contrast, the bottomland is critical to submerged landscape studies as it is evidence of the ancient landscape being investigated. While there is overlap between methods for both nautical and submerged landscape studies, this discussion will focus on the latter. Most sites underwater are like those we know from the terrestrial record and can be investigated accordingly. While the methods for site discovery are the most divergent, once sites are found, the sampling and excavating process is remarkably similar.

4.1 Finding Submerged Sites

Finding submerged sites is of course the most critical, and oftentimes, the most challenging first step. To begin, many sites are chance finds made by the public all over the world. Sponge divers finding shipwrecks in the Mediterranean is well known. The Doggerland paleontological fossils and archaeological materials found by fishers and beachcombers in and along the North Sea are another example. In eastern Asia, an archaic *Homo* fossil was recovered in a fishing net from the 60–120 m Penghu channel, 25 km off the western shore of Taiwan (Chang et al. 2015). In Lake Biwa, fishermen recovered stone spears and pottery, alerting archaeologists that artifacts from multiple time periods were submerged in the lake (Nakagawa 2014). Archaeological remains are often found by SCUBA divers, particularly in areas where recreational SCUBA is common, such as inland Florida, the Gulf of Mexico, and Mexican cenotes (Chatters et al. 2017; MacDonald et. al 2020). Oftentimes such finds serve as the starting point for systematic field research (e.g., Smith 2022). Just as farmers are instrumental in reporting archaeological sites on land, the support of those who live, work, and play in the world's waters has contributed to our knowledge of the past (Gaffney 2022).

In the search for sites, there is a general correlation between the age of a site and the material left behind, where the older a site is, the smaller the amount of material. This is a function of both postdepositional processes, that is, more time for organic materials to erode, degrade, and decompose, and the nature of human occupations; that is, mobile foragers create sites that are often ephemeral. This is compounded by working underwater where most detection techniques available are not designed for the scale of archaeological materials such as lithic artifacts or bone fragments, and the oldest sites are often in the deepest water, creating cost and logistic challenges. Overall, accessibility plays a large role in site discovery as expense and technological difficulty both increase with depth. Most submerged landscapes and sites have been found in relatively shallow water (less than 10 m) and in areas that often have good visibility and accessibility (Missiaen et al. 2017: 22–23). In addition to chance finds, systematic methods for finding submerged sites have been developed and are outlined here including the use of predictive models, direct search techniques, and acoustic surveys. Survey is used here for searching a site while site mapping or site documentation, the activities designed to record the character and spatial layout of a submerged site, are discussed in Section 4.2. As in all cases, scale in archaeology is an important consideration. Various scales of research from the region to the site can be outlined at three levels: macro-, meso-, and micro-. This is a useful heuristic for methods development and research designs, as different methods tend to work best or only at a certain scale (Figure 9).

4.1.1 Predictive Models

Archaeological fieldwork can be time consuming and expensive – more so in underwater environments. One means for narrowing search areas is predictive models, those that are based on a range of factors, applied to a specific region/ context, and used to hypothesize where sites are most likely to be found and

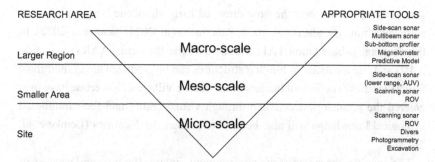

Figure 9 General schematic of the scales of research and the appropriate subsea tools and techniques for each level of investigation.

preserved. For submerged landscapes, most predictive models have sought to reconstruct the paleoenvironment as a baseline and then include factors related to subsistence strategies, often of foragers, to predict where sites may be located. While predictive models have had some success stories, one in particular, the "Danish Model", they are based on a range of assumptions often outlining "least cost" or "rational" behavior. If we have learned anything about human behavior, particular hunter-gatherer adaptations, it is that they rarely conform to our expectations (e.g., Anderson et al. 2023; Lemke 2018). However, with these considerations in mind, predictive models are useful tools that generate locations to be tested.

The "fishing site model" (Fischer 1993, 1995a, 1997, 2007) or "Danish Model" (Benjamin 2010), was based on interviews with Danish fishermen on the methods they used and species they fished for, then applied to the submerged topography/Mesolithic landscape. Essentially, ideal spots for catching fish remained remarkably similar from the Mesolithic to the twentieth century as animal behavior remained consistent. Even with sea level rise, prime fishing spots which fit the modeled parameters could be located underwater. Archaeological surveys targeting the locations predicted by the model discovered many sites, often two or three a day (Fischer 1993a, b, 1997). Areas outside of these fishing spots were also surveyed and did not recover archaeological materials, a critical test of this model, which concluded that prehistoric settlement was not random (Fischer 1993b, 1995). Benjamin (2010) adds additional steps for broader application, essentially outlining standard archaeological procedures (Table 1) to apply to submerged landscapes and Faught's (2010) use of "terrestrial analog modeling" has also proved successful (2002–2004, 2004, see also Faught and Smith 2021). In addition to the intuitive selection of research areas, work in the Great Lakes on 9,000-year-old hunting sites has utilized artificial intelligence (AI) agent-based modeling and computer simulation to reconstruct the now drowned early Holocene landscape and its associated biota (O'Shea et al. 2014; Palazzolo et al. 2021; Saad et al. 2022). In this case, agent-based model AI caribou transverse the virtual AAR (see section 3.4.2) and site locations of hunting structures can be predicted along their most traveled routes. Traditional hunters in the Native Village of Kotzebue have then entered the prehistoric landscape through virtual reality and their traditional ecological knowledge will also be used to predict site locations (Lemke et al. 2023).

The specific character of the environment dictates the type and success of modeling, and/or the intuitive selection of research areas. For example, visibility, rate/degree of sedimentation, water temperature, degree of scouring, marine wildlife, relative salinity, and other factors influence the degree to which archaeological materials will be visible during a survey and the ease and applicability of the different types of survey techniques outlined below.

4.1.2 Direct Search Techniques and Coring

Direct search techniques are possible, and for a known site or high-probability area, these may be the fastest means for targeted surveys. Direct search with divers is the most equivalent to ground survey. It covers the smallest total area but in the finest detail. SCUBA divers can conduct a direct survey by going underwater and swimming transects or using a motorized scooter to cover more ground and surface to collect artifacts (Figure 10). Snorkeling can also work in areas of shallow water. Good visibility is paramount for all direct search techniques. Obviously, the most significant limitation of a direct diver survey is the amount of time divers can stay underwater to conduct the search. Total bottom time is related to many variables including working depth, diver fitness, water temperature, gas mix, etc. Drawbacks include the reliance on good visibility, not just in the water column itself but on the seafloor as well, as many artifacts can become encrusted and/or obscured by marine growth, including invasive species, and chemical reactions (Section 5). Diver survey only covers a small area and there can be difficulties in locating the areas searched, as GPS underwater is still in its infancy; however, reference lines and grids can help. Overall, direct search with divers in the least technologically demanding. There are important logistics to keep in mind with SCUBA of course, such as the optimal number of divers, the tradeoff between increased coverage and working efficiency (i.e., covering more ground faster), the capabilities of the support vessel, ensuring divers have the appropriate certifications and training, and emergency planning.

Figure 10 A diver bags an early stage lithic preform from the Clint's Scallop Hole site, Apalachee Bay, Gulf of Mexico, off the coast of north Florida, USA. Photograph courtesy of Morgan F. Smith.

In order to survey for longer periods of time, direct search can be conducted with ROVs or submarines. ROVs can range in size and specifications with different accessories and tools, but even small hand-deployable options can conduct direct searches as live video is sent back to a surface unit via a cable. ROVs are limited by available power on the vessel or battery life but in either case, they can far exceed the average time of open-circuit SCUBA divers on the bottom. They are still not an equivalent substitute for human divers, however. Indeed, ROVs and SCUBA divers can work in tandem, as the ROV can record the coordinates of survey transects and finds (since the ROV is connected to the surface vessel and it's GPS location). Ideally, ROV pilots will be fluent in dive signs and hand signals so SCUBA divers can communicate with the surface vessel via the live video feed from the ROV. Submarines can also transport archaeologists to the bottom where direct search can then be conducted, but this is the most expensive and equipment-intensive option.

Direct search techniques also include coring and sampling and can function as the equivalent of shovel tests, although much more technologically demanding. Coring is common during offshore work for recording sedimentological, environmental, and archaeological data. Coring is crucial in areas with thick sedimentation where archaeological sites may be deeply buried, such as the Gulf of Mexico (Evans and Keith 2011). Although a small window into buried layers, core analysis can identify peat deposits, shell middens, provide organics for radiocarbon dating, and occasionally lithic or other artifacts. Locating mircodebitage in cores proved a useful approach in Canadian lakes as the microscopic remains of flintknapping leave a "cloud" around large artifacts that are more likely to be discovered in coring operations (Sonnenburg et al. 2011). Depending on the size of the core, depth of the water, and depth of the cored sediment, coring operations can require industrial research vessels and intensive coring equipment. On a much smaller scale, ponars (geological grab samplers), can be lowered from a surface vessel onto the seafloor to take a sample of bottom sediments. This can be used for paleoenvironmental recon-structions and for ground-truthing SONAR surveys; however, their direct applicability to archaeological goals is limited as the samplers do not maintain stratigraphy, and recording the precise location of the sample is difficult. While cores are often utilized to search for evidence of past human activity, they can also be used as a means of limited excavation, primarily to record stratigraphy. In either use, proper analysis of cores is essential and requires specialized techniques and skillsets, core scanners are ideal as well as geoarchaeological interpretation and the ability to recognize inundated terrestrial sediments.

4.1.3 Acoustic Techniques

Remote sensing underwater comes in a range of forms and is equivalent to remote sensing on land. Techniques include examining visual imagery such as aerial or satellite images and acoustic techniques. Shipwrecks can often be seen in aerial images as they are large and unique enough from the surrounding bottom sedi-ments or objects. Green lidar can penetrate shallow water depths and has detected shipwrecks (e.g., Shih et al. 2013) and may be very useful in the future for mapping submerged sites and/or landscapes. Metal detection similar to terrestrial survey can be performed via a magnetometer underwater. Magnetometers have been extremely useful in detecting sites of underwater cultural heritage such as ship and aircraft wrecks and can also be used to characterize geological features on the seafloor, although in general, they are less useful when searching for prehistoric sites dating before widespread metal use.

By far the most systematic research methods for finding submerged sites involve acoustic search techniques and surveys. Like a terrestrial survey, a search area is designated, transect spacing is selected and then the area is covered. Just as on land, these methods serve to find and map archaeological sites, guide further investigation including excavation, and are nondestructive/noninvasive. Survey planning includes selecting the appropriate search techniques given the nature of the search area (topography, depth, temperature, distance offshore, topside weather, available surface support vessel, etc.) and time and cost parameters of the project. The most critical aspects of surveying submerged landscapes are the factors of scale and environment. Approaches vary depending on the target. For a nautical archaeology project, one would be likely to conduct a targeted search, versus submerged landscape studies where you would conduct a continuous coverage survey. In designing the survey, considerations are given to establish the expected character of the site (if known), such as physical characteristics and postdepositional processes that may have impacted it. For example, the continental shelves vary widely from buried to exposed features, sandy or rocky bottoms, hard or soft sediments, the presence of caves, etc. (Missiaen et al. 2017: 22). Matching the appropriate technique for the target is critical. Does the technique have the necessary resolution needed? Will it perform well with the expected environmental setting including depth and surface conditions? Matching the technique to the research budget includes factoring in the price to purchase or rent a platform and the cost of post-survey processing if outsourced. The time it takes to do the survey and processing must also be budgeted as some techniques are faster than others. Other survey specifications include the range and frequency used (e.g., side-scan SONAR has variable ranges and can operate in both high and low frequency, see Atherton 2011), the search pattern, the percentage of transect overlap, and the planned vessel speed (ideal speed for most acoustic techniques is as slow as possible while still maintaining a straight course/transect and forward momentum). Ultimately, designing a survey is entirely dependent on the types of targets you are searching for as well as operational logistics.

Side-scan SONAR and multibeam echo sounders are the most used acoustic instruments for seafloor mapping and underwater archaeological surveys where paleolandscapes are exposed or shallowly buried. Side-scan is an active SONAR system that detects and images objects on the seafloor/lakebed. The physical sensors of the SONAR, the transducers, are located on either side, and these send and receive pulses of sound that map the seafloor and other objects resting on the bottom. Side-scan creates an image of large areas and can detect differences in material type and texture of the seabed. Transducer arrays can be mounted on a ship's hull, or on another platform such as a towfish or an AUV. Many side-scan SONAR arrays are on towfish and they are connected to the vessel via a cable to a topside unit that displays the data in real time and records it. GPS coordinates are collected most often via the boat and offsets and layback are calculated (the distance between the GPS receiver and the towfish, the depth of the towfish, and the amount of cable out). With the appropriate calculations, targets of interest seen on side-scan imagery can be precisely located and investigated further. Multibeam SONAR is also an active SONAR system used to map the seafloor. Unlike a single-beam system, it deploys multiple SONAR beams at the same time in a fan-shaped pattern and covers a wide swath. Multibeam produces two data streams, sea floor depth and backscatter imagery, which can provide information about the geological makeup of the seafloor. When conducting multibeam operations, sound casts are completed to record the speed of sound in the water in the local area (which varies with salinity, temperature, etc.). This is then used to calculate the travel time from the transducers to the seafloor and back. Both side-scan and multibeam SONAR can be deployed from small boats and in increasingly shallow water (Figures 11 and 12a–b, Sakellariou et al. 2011).

While side-scan and multibeam map the seafloor surface, sub-bottom profiling, a method of sub-seafloor mapping, is critical for detecting buried features. Ideal targets for sub-bottom profiling include buried paleochannel features, shell middens, wooden remains, and peat deposits which often preserve organic remains and can indicate past shorelines (although the latter produces biogenic gas which can

Figure 11 An autonomous underwater vehicle equipped with side-scan SONAR operated off a 7.6 m Parker, *S/V Blue Traveler*, Lake Huron, Great Lakes, USA. Photograph by the author.

(a)

(b)

Figure 12 Multibeam SONAR installed on a 6.4 m Parker, Traverse Bay, Lake Michigan, Great Lakes, USA. **(a)** View of the M3 Multibeam SONAR Portable Hydrographic System, Kongsberg. This multibeam system is designed for shallow water applications not to exceed 50 m in depth. **(b)** Overview images of the SONAR and the vessel. Photographs by the author.

obscure the seismic results [Missiaen et al. 2017: 27; Plets et al. 2007]). Small, buried features and individual artifacts are extremely difficult to identify although past projects have recorded successful incidences of locating lithic artifacts by their differential resonance patterns as they appear on sub-bottom (Grøn et al. 2018, 2021; Hermand et al. 2011; Morris et al. 2022; Ren et al. 2011). It is critical to note that these technologies are fast evolving, and it can be difficult to acquire the latest models, particularly given the budgetary constraint of archaeology. Furthermore, these technologies were not designed with archaeology in mind but rather were created for entirely different purposes such as geological studies or military applications (Missiaen et al. 2017: 22). Developing specific, purpose-designed prospection tools for submerged landscapes is important as most of the instruments used thus far are commercial off the shelf. All acoustic surveys can be georeferenced and added to GIS systems, and the same search area can be covered using multiple techniques. One of the greatest assets of acoustic techniques is their ability to generate detailed visuals in areas of low visibility. As these techniques use sound rather than light to create images, they are not hampered by dark, low-visibility water, which impacts divers and other direct search methods.

4.2 Mapping Submerged Sites

While the first step is to find submerged sites, the second is to map them and assess the type of site, its size, and layout. Site documentation after finding a site but before excavation is a critical step for archaeologists working in any environment, but this is especially true underwater as visibility may be obscured after sampling or excavation starts. As with finding submerged sites, there are a range of methods for mapping them, including direct methods by SCUBA divers to remote methods, both robotic and acoustic. Again, all of these techniques can be conducted at a single site and the data combined for the most accurate and representative image.

4.2.1 Diver Plan Maps

Similar to diver survey, diver plan maps are among the least technologically challenging, they can be done with or without an overlaying grid and most are completed by hand using a pencil on mylar paper, or on transparent acrylic sheets with a wax pencil (Figures 13 and 14). Plan maps underwater are completed with a compass and tape just as on land. While a cheap and fairly easy method of direct observation, plan maps are reliant on good visibility, artistic skill, ability to measure accurately, and sufficient bottom time. Diver maps can then be digitized. Other methods of diving, in addition to SCUBA include surface-supplied air where air is sent to divers working in shallow depths via long, flexible hoses from

Figure 13 Diver Adam Burke maps an in situ flintknapping deposit at the Clint's Scallop Hole site, Apalachee Bay, Gulf of Mexico, off the coast of north Florida, USA. Photograph courtesy of Morgan F. Smith.

Figures 14 Diver recording cairn markers in submerged caves in Yucatán Peninsula, Quintana Roo, México. Photograph courtesy of El Centro Investigador del Sistema Acuífero de Quintana Roo A.C. (CINDAQ).

the surface. Less bulky and longer lasting than SCUBA tanks, surface-supplied divers can stay down the longer times needed for careful mapping and excavating. Large-scale projects just as Port Royal and the detailed excavation at Page-Ladson and other sites in Florida have been completed using surface-supplied air. Such methods work well once sites have been found, since during survey divers need flexibility to cover large areas and would be hampered by surface-connected hoses. While in the past entire sites, cities, and shipwrecks were plan drawn by divers (or snorkelers if shallow enough), in great detail – large-scale sites and features can be more quickly and accurately mapped using photogrammetry or remote methods.

4.2.2 Photogrammetry

Photogrammetry has created precise, three-dimensional maps and images of archaeological sites and landscapes. The resulting high-precision data allow for post-processing measuring or "virtual fieldwork" (Missiaen et al. 2017: 32) of sites and features as well as correct texture and color (McCarthy and Benjamin 2014). Photogrammetric models of cultural features and sites have been particularly successful at mapping submerged caves in México, such as the submerged red ochre mines in Quintana Roo (MacDonald et al. 2020) and paleontological/archaeological investigations at Hoyo Negro (Rissolo et al. 2015). In these settings, technical diving is required, and detailed photogrammetry allows specialists such as biological anthropologists (who may not have the required diving certifications) to complete their analyses digitally. Furthermore, caves are difficult to survey and map using traditional seafloor mapping techniques as these are based on plan view projection, and are not suitable for vertical walls (Missiaen et al. 2017: 34). Therefore, photogrammetry and other forms of scanning have been instrumental in these settings. Overall photogrammetry is useful as another means of direct observation, as it's fairly fast and accurate. Drawbacks are limited but include the dependence on good visibility or the use of artificial lighting, and software costs/processing time.

4.2.3 Remotely Operated Vehicles

ROVs can be used for site mapping both in video and with acoustic methods depending on the payload. For example, an Outland 1000 ROV has been used extensively to investigate targets selected during geophysical surveys in the Great Lakes and to map identified archaeological sites and features. Plan maps can be generated from ROV video if the ROV is equipped with scale bars as stills from the video can then be scaled and oriented using the ROV's compass (Figure 15). ROVs can also be equipped with their own

Figure 15 Outland 1000 remotely operated vehicle (ROV) *Jake* equipped for submerged site survey and mapping on the Alpena-Amberley Ridge, Lake Huron, Great Lakes, USA. Two red laser pointers installed on the front of the ROV provide scale. Photograph by the author.

acoustic sensors depending on the size and scale of the ROV. Optional additions include side-scan, scanning SONARs, sub-bottom profilers, etc. Forward-looking SONARs in particular are useful in areas of poor visibility. ROVs can also be loaded with pinging SONARs or locating SONARs that give their real-time GPS coordinates, which helps in relocating archaeological sites and features and recording sample and/or unit locations (see section 4.3.3).

4.2.4 Scanning SONAR

Scanning SONAR can be used to find sites (O'Shea et al. 2014) but more often is used to map known sites. A technique developed for industry, such as bridge and dam inspections, scanning SONARs can operate on any standard PC using a Windows-based application (Atherton 2011). The SONAR rests within a tripod which is lowered near the target and a rotating transducer creates a live feed acoustic image to the topside unit. Various settings include frequency, range, and SONAR speed. Compass lock and scaling rings can quickly measure sites and features (Figure 16). As with any other acoustic method, one of the most

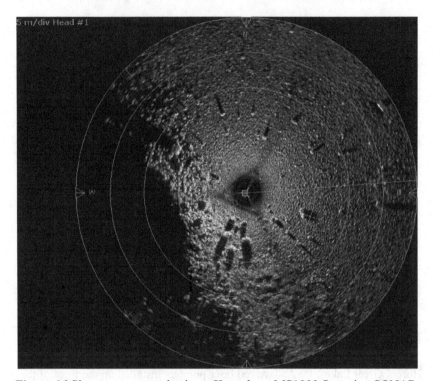

Figure 16 Site map generated using a Kongsberg MS1000 Scanning SONAR, submerged prehistoric archaeological site, built stone structure (near center), Lake Huron, Great Lakes, USA. Scaling rings are 5 m increments, depth is 32 m. Image provided by the author.

significant applications of scanning SONAR for mapping archaeological sites is in the context of low visibility. It is also extremely fast and once deployed, can map sites accurately within minutes. Multiple SONAR drops can be done and their resulting images combined to map larger areas.

4.2.5 Autonomous Underwater Vehicles

AUVs can be equipped with an array of sensors, including side-scan SONAR, cameras, etc. AUVs are useful for a number of reasons. Since they are not connected to the boat like a traditional towfish and have their own GPS systems, layback does not need to be calculated and they are not as susceptible to surface conditions, waves, etc. as towfish (although they are not immune to these factors). With their own propulsion and navigation, and unhampered by a tether, they can fly closer to the bottom creating higher-resolution images. Survey time is reliant on battery life and unlike using a towfish, the data are not displayed in real time. Instead, it is downloaded off of the AUV once it has returned from its mission.

AUVs with side-scan have been successfully employed to map submerged land-scapes and sites in the Great Lakes (Figures 17 and 18) and micro-AUVs are starting to be used for archaeological mapping.

Importantly, methods for both finding and mapping submerged archaeological sites can be combined to create the most accurate images and maps, not only in terms of measurement, but also color, texture, and environmental setting. Large-scale mapping can be done first at high ranges and low frequency, using either side-scan and/or multibeam to get a general sense of the seafloor and any features on the surface in large areas. These same areas can also be surveyed with a sub-bottom profiler to ascertain any sub-seafloor features. Once smaller areas of interest, or microregions (O'Shea 2021) are identified, a side-scan SONAR survey can be dialed in at a more refined scale with lower ranges and high frequency and/or closer to the bottom for higher resolution using an AUV. Within microregions, once targets of interest are identified, ROV video and SONAR documentation can be completed as well as scanning SONAR images of the sites and features in addition to SCUBA diver plan maps and photogram-metric modeling (e.g., O'Shea 2015; O'Shea and Lemke 2020) (see Figure 9). All of these layers can be managed using GIS.

Figure 17 An Iver 3, Ocean Server Technology autonomous underwater vehicle (AUV) on the surface before diving and conducting a side-scan SONAR survey of submerged archaeological sites on the Alpena-Amberley Ridge, Lake Huron, Great Lakes, USA. Photograph by the author.

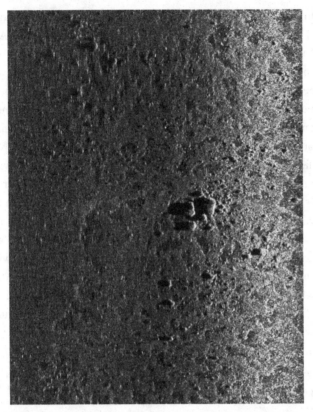

Figure 18 Side-scan SONAR image collected by an Iver 3 Ocean Server Technology autonomous underwater vehicle (AUV) at an altitude of 6 m above the bottom. Submerged prehistoric archaeological site, built stone structure (center right), Lake Huron, Great Lakes, USA. Depth is 32 m, largest rock is 1 m long. Image provided by the author.

4.3 Excavating Submerged Sites

After submerged sites are discovered and mapped, data recovery and analysis proceed. Excavating underwater has its own challenges and surface and sub-surface sampling can be completed ranging from limited sampling to total site excavation. Total site excavation provides a complete picture, ensures that site materials are available for scientific investigation, and allows for the fullest range of potential questions to be investigated. However, it is effort-intensive, expensive, leaves nothing for future investigations, and may produce redundant information. Furthermore, it creates a massive legacy of materials which require conservation, which is not inconsequential as waterlogged materials require special techniques (see Section 5). This is one of the reasons that the UNESCO

2001 Convention suggests in situ preservation and conservation as a first option (Section 5). While total site excavation is not recommended, site testing and limited excavation are essential for many research goals and are dependent upon research questions. Methods for underwater excavation are detailed extensively elsewhere, although many of these focus on shipwrecks (e.g., Bowens 2008; Green 2016; Klyuev et al. 2023). Here, methods are outlined using three options for digging submerged sites, (1) removing the water and excavating the sites as terrestrial, (2) excavating underwater using airlifts or water dredges, and (3) remote and robotic sampling.

4.3.1 Cofferdams and Creating "Dry" Submerged Sites

Excavating underwater has its own challenges, including the length of time archaeologists can spend on the bottom digging (although surface-supplied air works well for longer periods of time). One solution to this and other challenges has been to drain water off of submerged sites using various methods to create "dry" sites that can then be excavated using traditional techniques. Cofferdams are the most common method and have been used to essentially make underwater sites terrestrial. Some of the more notable cofferdam excavations have been in the realm of nautical archaeology including La Salle's ship *La Belle* and the Skuldelev Viking ships (Bruseth 2014; Olsen and Crumlin-Pedersen 1968). Depending on the size of the site and water depth, cofferdams can present a significant investment in engineering. Furthermore, completely removing water from submerged sites and materials too fast, or allowing them to completely dry out, can lead to disastrous results, particularly as organic materials become exposed to air and begin to degrade. Even within cofferdams materials are kept moist while being excavated. In terms of submerged prehistory, cofferdams were used to excavate shallower sites in Lake Biwa, Japan including the Awazu shell midden (see section 3.4.1) which rested in 2–3 m below water. A cofferdam of double-rowed iron sheet piles filled with sediment was constructed around the site and then water was pumped out (Nakagawa 2014).

Aside from cofferdams, experiments in draining the water out of cenotes have been conducted. In the Maya area, early underwater archaeological investigations of the Chichén Itzá and Chinkultic cenotes attempted to drain the water out so they could then be excavated as dry land. However, the pumps were unable to keep up with the amount of water pouring into the cenotes from the water table and water was never entirely removed. While water levels were lowered, excavation was still difficult given the steep sides of the cenotes and the nature of the ritual deposits, which had created a palimpsest of items from many different episodes and lacked clear stratigraphy (Andrews and Corletta 1995: 111).

4.3.2 Underwater Excavation

Many excavations have been conducted underwater, often utilizing airlifts or water dredges (Figure 19). In airlifts, air under pressure is introduced at the bottom of a tube. As the air rises up the tube, it expands and creates suction at the base of the tube. Sediment is then lifted up from the bottom and collected beyond the upper end of the tube. Airlifts can be used alongside hand fanning to lift up sediments from the bottom and away from artifacts being sucked up the tube. Essentially, hand fanning and airlifts (or water dredges, see below) are used to remove sediment from around artifacts as troweling and buckets would do on land. In shallower settings, sediments from the airlift are either sent up to a platform usually straight to screens, or up to a boat to be collected. In deeper water, airlifted sediments are caught in a mesh bag in the water column, which essentially screens the matrix while artifacts in the bag are then recovered, or into a bucket and then lifted to the surface and retrieved (Figure 20). Sediments can then be transported back to controlled laboratory settings to be sieved. The water depth is critical, as in shallower settings the airlift tube can reach from the seafloor where excavation is happening up to a surface platform or vessel, while in deeper

Figure 19 Divers excavating a Mesolithic shell layer in the shallow waters off Hjarnø, Denmark. Photograph courtesy of Jonathan Benjamin, (after Astrup et al. 2019).

Figure 20 Airlifted sediments collected in two, nineteen-liter buckets at depth, raised to the surface using a lift bag from excavations at submerged archaeological sites 30 m below water, Alpena-Amberley Ridge, Lake Huron, Great Lakes, USA. Photograph by the author.

waters it is not feasible for the airlift tube to go all the way to the surface, nor would proper suction work over that distance. Just as on land, general methods are adapted for specific sites, and similar to terrestrial archaeology, not all methods will work at different sites. For example, an airlift that was designed to excavate submerged sites in Florida's karstic sinkholes and rivers was used in Lake Huron and froze given the dramatic differences in water temperature.

Similar to an airlift, a water dredge is a long tube with a dredge head. High-pressure water is injected at a bend and is directed so flow is axial with the long pipe. This induces suction at the base of the tube. Flexible materials can be added at the working end to increase mobility. Excavations at Port Royal were completed using a water dredge (Hamilton 1984: 16). Comparing the two techniques, airlifts typically run on low air pressure, which may be a problem in shallower water (works best below 5 m). Other considerations include the fact that the lift tube is buoyant and needs to be anchored and weighted, but it can be highly portable with compressed gas cylinders, and the vertical attitude of the pipe integrates well with screens. Water dredges run on high-pressure water so they are useful at shallow depths, but the tube must be maintained near-horizontal attitude, which limits downward excavation and/or upward dispersal of overburden and its efficiency decreases as the length of the tube increases. Lastly, it requires a high-pressure water compressor, which requires surface support (Figures 21a–b and 22). While airlifts and water dredges

Figure 21 Both sides of excavations using a water dredge, **(a)** Divers Jessi Halligan (right) and David Thulman (left) piece plot artifacts at the Ryan-Harley site, a Paleoindian-aged site in the Wacissa River, north Florida, USA, **(b)** Ed Green (left) and Morgan Smith (right) monitor the screen during a Florida afternoon thunderstorm on a barge to collect dredged sediment from Ryan-Harley. Sediment passes through 1/4 inch and 1/16 inch screens. Photographs courtesy of Morgan F. Smith.

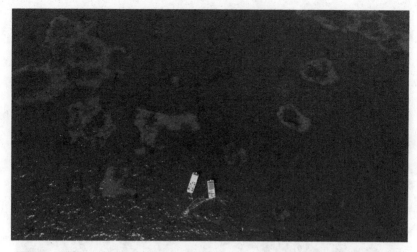

Figure 22 Excavation and site mapping underwater at a newly discovered archaeological locality in the Gulf of Mexico, off the coast of Florida, USA. Light patches are archaeological sites. Dark areas are seagrasses. Photograph courtesy of Morgan F. Smith.

remove the matrix and can recover artifacts in the screens, other materials need to be brought to the surface. Methods for recovering artifacts vary from direct transport by the diver to the use of lift bags, ROVs, and cranes in the case of very heavy objects.

4.3.3 Robotic Sampling

While ROVs are mostly limited to video recording of the surficial features, they can be equipped with manipulators. Still, most ROVs cannot excavate (Missiaen et al. 2017); but small ROVs have been used to collect environmental samples such as macrobotanical remains, including small sticks and twigs, and samples of submerged peat deposits. While it does not have the capability to excavate or collect heavy samples, collecting organic remains via a robotic arm is extremely useful for ancient and environmental DNA (aeDNA) research by limiting contamination, which may occur with SCUBA diver collected samples. Additionally, ROVs can be used to record site locations and excavation units using a GPS transponder (Figure 23).

Any excavation of submerged sites and the controlled recovery of artifacts and sampled materials begins with data recording. Recording underwater must be clear and standardized, as often the individual who is recovering and labeling artifacts below water will not be the same person who receives the objects on the surface. Additionally, the individual analyzing materials in a laboratory may not

Figure 23 Outland 1000 remotely operated vehicle (ROV) *Jake* recording the location of the excavation unit 15 at Drop 45, a submerged archaeological site on the Alpena-Amberley Ridge, Lake Huron, Great Lakes, USA (O'Shea et al. 2014). Photograph provided by the author.

have directly observed the site. The system must have built-in redundancy with artifact labels, divers' logs, in-water plan drawings, pre-lifting photography/photogrammetry/video recording ideally with the labels visible (Figure 24), and a surface and sample log. There should also be immediate post-dive review and recording. Essentially all the same basic rules which apply to excavations on land apply underwater, too. Any project investigating submerged sites needs to have proper plans and procedures in place for recovering and conserving the unique data found in these types of environments, particularly organic remains which require careful recovery and specialized care.

5 Types of Data: Material Culture, Resurfaced

Generally, as illustrated above, underwater sites are noted for their excellent preservation which tends to preserve archaeological materials much better than terrestrial soils, leaving submerged data qualitatively different than terrestrial. Taking just one site, Tybrind Vig, as an example, over 60 percent of the assemblage was organic, including many artifacts and entire classes of data that have never been found in terrestrial Mesolithic sites (Andersen 2013). Lithic artifacts, human and animal bones, wooden objects, and many other archaeological remains have been recovered from diverse underwater

Figure 24 Diver labeling pieces of a Mesolithic wood platform at Bouldnor Cliff, Solent, United Kingdom. Photograph courtesy of Garry Momber.

settings, including high-energy coastlines, low-energy environments in the open sea, and in shallow as well as deep water (Bailey 2014). Admittedly, one of the standard hallmarks of archaeology underwater is the presence of unique data.

5.1 Unique Data

What is so special about submerged sites and landscapes? The type of data found at submerged sites includes stellar organic preservation, environmental proxies, novel evidence, and data at different temporal and spatial scales – all of which can supplement the terrestrial record.

While underwater contexts vary in salinity, temperature, currents, wave action, biogenic life, etc., preservation overall is extraordinary. Preservation only increases with distance away from the equator as colder waters can essentially freeze archaeological sites and materials, have less light, and less aquatic life impacting organic remains. Since the material culture of most societies past and present is largely organic, the differential preservation of wood, leather, bone, fiber, textiles, and plants underwater helps correct the bias found in the archaeological record toward durable, inorganic materials. Large quantities of organic remains can revolutionize our knowledge about past societies. Floral and faunal assemblages provide detailed information about the past environment, but also about past subsistence practices. For example, the Awazu shell midden below Lake Biwa demonstrated a change in the type of nuts used by Jomon foragers (Iba 2005) and it has been well-documented that submerged data from the Baltic have revolutionized our understanding of Mesolithic forager-fishers (Astrup 2018).

While for shipwrecks the bottom is largely irrelevant, for submerged land-scapes, studies of the seafloor are essential as that is the terrestrial surface that was previously exposed and occupied. Mapping of the bottomlands becomes critical for understanding the topography of the prehistoric land surface as well as environmental features such as boulder fields, marshes, bogs, rivers, streams, peat deposits, etc. Sampling of the seafloor and sub-seafloor can be used to recover environmental indicators such as marcobotanical remains, pollen, phyto-liths, diatoms, testate amoebae, and aeDNA (e.g., Sonnenburg and O'Shea 2017) (Figure 25). Many of these environmental indicators are complementary and independent datasets, which can outline the environment at different spatial scales including the site-level, immediate area, local region, and the larger landscape. The preservation of such environmental evidence allows for paleoenvironmental reconstructions, further aiding predictive models and interpretations of past land use. In many cases, the paleoenvironments of submerged landscapes are novel climates that are very different from those seen in the same areas today.

Given the range of site types that exist underwater (Section 3), data from submerged sites can speak to different temporal and spatial scales. For example, there are single component sites such as Manasota Key in Florida

Figure 25 A sample of peat collected from the Alpena-Amberley Ridge, Lake Huron, Great Lakes, USA, dating to 9,500 cal yr BP with preserved pollen and macrobotanical remains. Photograph by the author.

which are contrasted by deep, stratigraphic deposits with diachronic records such as Page-Ladson, also in Florida. Spatial scales of investigation can also vary underwater between site-level investigations such as Flying Foam Shoals in Australia or Bouldnor Cliff in England (Benjamin et al. 2020; Momber et al. 2011), and regional settlement pattern analyses such as those conducted on the AAR in Lake Huron and Mesolithic sites in the Baltic (Astrup 2018; O'Shea 2021). Regional settlement patterns are particularly useful underwater, as a series of sites can be investigated with their spatial relationships intact due to limited postdepositional disturbance and no subsequent human occupation. Such patterns on land are often obscured or missing sites.

Some data found underwater are from time periods that are unknown and/or poorly understood from terrestrial records. For example, the preserved food remains from Lake Biwa provide evidence of sophisticated nut processing and the importance of nuts, fish, and animals in the subsistence regime during the Jomon period (Habu et al. 2011; Iba 2005). Nut husks, and fish and animal bones from this time period quickly decompose on land. It was previously believed that Jomon subsistence focused largely on hunting, but the underwater evidence demonstrates that fishing and foraging were critical to Jomon lifeways. The Awazu shell midden is a unique case as the organic data it preserved contributed to the study of not just aquatic food but terrestrial food as well (Habu et al. 2011: 25). Higashimyo is another site in Japan that has a complex story revealed by stratigraphy. A Jomon shell midden that was submerged by rising water levels, today the site is buried under an alluvial deposit and Jomon occupations are capped by a marine clay deposit which preserved Initial Jomon organic materials. This preservation provides the oldest evidence of substantial wood-working and basket-making in the Jomon period (Habu 2011: 24–25). While Lake Biwa provides unique evidence of past lifeways little known from the terrestrial record, similarly the sites below Lake Huron are among the oldest dated hunting architecture sites in the world thus far, extending the use of such structures into the early Holocene (Lemke 2022). While these sites represent time periods poorly known from the terrestrial record, there are also certain items that are not likely to be discarded on land, such as valuables, heirlooms, etc. that can be found underwater, particularly in catastrophic sites that were not intentionally abandoned (Martin 2020).

Importantly, data from submerged sites can be a complement to data from the terrestrial record. A holistic view of the past requires data from both sides of the waterline, particularly in coastal or nearshore areas. These landscapes are dynamic and people have been living on them for thousands or tens of thousands of years, making connections between the terrestrial and submerged records critical for understanding the past. If we only studied harbors and ports that are dry land now, how can we know if those sites are typical (Flemming 1971: xiv)? Without going underwater and exploring the whole range of ports and harbors, we cannot know what an outlier is, and thus what may be skewing our interpretations. The same is true for all types of sites – if we only investigated sites that are dry now and were far inland then, how would we know what early coastal settlement was like? How can we be assured of the relative accuracy of our interpretations of past lifeways? In some cases, data that are not available on land may be found underwater. In other cases, we may be missing part of the subsistence regime by only looking underwater or only looking on land, as has been exampled in the Baltic, Lake Biwa, and the Great Lakes. In other cases, we can extend human use of the coastlines back thousands of years, such as in Australia and Doggerland and extend the timing of human occupation in certain regions such as North American as evidenced at the Page-Ladson site. As archaeologists, our models about the past are incomplete at best if we do not look at landscapes we know humans inhabited, and capture the novel data they have preserved. Given the theoretical grounding presented in Section 2, and the tools outlined in Section 4, archaeologists are well equipped to explore submerged sites and landscapes and reveal their unique data about the past. In searching for such data, we must be mindful of the special conservation factors that come into play.

5.2 Conservation

Conservation is a science that is crucial for archaeology. This is a field of practice that requires specialized training and techniques in chemistry and materials science, as well as collaboration with archaeologists and heritage practitioners. For underwater archaeologists, conservation is a special concern given the wide array of materials that are preserved in underwater settings. The exceptional preservation of materials from underwater sites does not mean that archaeological conservation and preservation are easier, in fact, these objects require special care to remain in their well-preserved state. When immersed for long periods, artifacts react chemically with both water and surrounding sediments. One of the most important conservation issues for underwater archaeologists is the sudden removal of objects from water and their resulting exposure to air. This can set off a chain reaction of chemical and physical reactions in the artifact which can lead to its degradation, deterioration, or ultimate destruction. For these reasons, the conservation of waterlogged and submerged artifacts is unique enough to warrant a specific branch of conservation science (Björdal 2000; Maarleveld 2020; Memet 2008; Pearson 1987) and international best practices outlined by the 2001 UNESCO Convention state that in situ preservation should be considered the first option. Many in situ conservation practices have been developed (Björdal et al. 2012; Gregory and Matthiesen 2012; Richards and McKinnon 2010). These sites and materials are then monitored periodically to review their condition and possible removal if they are being damaged (e.g., the site is being eroded or otherwise disturbed/damaged). In general, artifacts should only be removed from their in situ context if there are valid research objectives that cannot be achieved otherwise. If removed, preservation begins from the moment of recovery.

Conservation works to preserve artifacts for research and display, and the conservation process often takes much longer than the excavation and removal of objects from sites. The long-term care of submerged artifacts is an expensive and time-consuming process that also requires specific storage facilities. Methods of conserving archaeological data and materials from underwater sites have been extensively covered by Hamilton, who reviews general procedures for the laboratory and field and conservation of bone, ivory, teeth, antler, pottery, glass, wood, leather, textiles, and metals (1976, 1996, 1999).

In almost all settings, including underwater, stone preserves well and other than washing it to stop salt crystals from forming on the surface (in saltwater environments, Muckelroy 1980: 180), does not need special conservation treatment or care. Wood and other organic objects represent a different problem. Waterlogged wood is a very common material found in submerged sites and when in its submerged context, natural resins within the wood are replaced by water. When still in situ this replacement by water does not dramatically alter the wood's original shape, appearance, or texture. When removed and if allowed to dry, without the water the cellular structure loses all of its internal support and will collapse, so the artifact shrinks, alters, warps, and in some cases deteriorates completely. Therefore, upon immediate removal, providing the most stable environment for waterlogged artifacts is key to their preservation, such as keeping wooden objects wet before they can be conserved. For example, in the case of submerged tree stumps/rooted trees or large pieces of waterlogged wood, rather than recovering the entire objects, a small sample can be removed for absolute dating (e.g., radiocarbon or dendrochronology) and identification, while the rest can remain in situ. Even these small pieces need to be kept either wet or, if being sent for dating, allowed to dry slowly. When entire wood objects are removed for research purposes, ideally the conservation treatment will preserve the original appearance, shape, dimensions, and surface feature; but just in case of alteration, photographs, drawings, photogrammetry, and detailed study of surficial features should happen immediately.

In practice, there is no perfect preservation technique. Each has its own drawbacks and there are no universally applicable methods. Just as on land, general practices must be adapted to local circumstances. The first reliable conservation process for waterlogged wood – and one of the most common methods – is using polyethylene glycol (PEG) (Hamilton 1999). PEG has proved useful and has been employed many times since it was introduced in the 1960s, including to treat some of the world's most famous shipwrecks such as the *Vasa*, although it can degrade over time (Mortensen et al. 2007). In addition to PEG there are many other processes for conserving wood including freeze-drying and the range of solutions available provides many options for conservators working on materials from different sites with different concerns (Hamilton 1999).

Metals are unique in that unlike organic objects, the preservation of metals underwater is not always exponentially better than on land. Chemical processes, particularly in salt water, can lead to corrosion and degradation. Concretions tend to form around metal objects obscuring the artifacts encased within them. These concretions can form relatively quickly, and chemical reactions will continue to occur when the object is removed from the underwater environment (Maarleveld 2020). Various metals react differently to both underwater environments and conservation treatments. In general, the problem-solving aspect of conservation, the range of techniques used, and the lengthy procedures involved are what distinguish conservation as its own unique science. Overall, properly conserving underwater materials requires funds for conservation, adequate and appropriate laboratory and curation space, and a specialized conservator, and these steps must be factored into archaeological projects from inception.

5.3 Interpretation

One of the most significant features of submerged sites is the data they preserve, which, with special care can be recovered and conserved. The array of site types found below water (Section 3) offers a range of data for addressing research questions. The types of questions asked of these data are directly related to the theoretical orientation and disciplinary focus of individual underwater archaeologists. Importantly, underwater archaeologists can collaborate with each other, as well as geological scientists, computer scientists, paleodemographers, paleoenvironmentalists, and conservators to allow their data to speak to the broadest range of issues. In terms of data from submerged sites, one area that is sorely lacking is taphonomy. While taphonomic studies are common for terrestrial sites and materials, we know surprisingly little about the impact of different matrices on waterlogged materials, the chemical processes which may alter them underwater, and how effects change over time. Without these studies differentiating between natural and cultural modifications of artifacts can be difficult.

Whether on land or underwater, archaeologists seek to infer the past from archaeological remains, acknowledging that the practice of archaeological interpretation is inherently probabilistic and there is the problem of equifinality. Archaeological conclusions are inherently probabilistic. Archaeological and historical explanations can be made with differing levels of confidence or certainty, and there is always the potential for the discovery of new evidence, which can alter explanations or identifications. The goal of understanding site formation (Section 3) and the unique character of the data is to maximize what we can say with certainty about the past.

6 The Future of the Underwater Past

Archaeology underwater is flourishing. It is an exciting specialty that can generate novel data about the past and aid us in answering some of our biggest questions about human behavior. Keeping in mind that new sites are being discovered every year, this Element has just provided a sample of the types of projects that are currently being conducted and the sites and data they are investigating. The sheer number of submerged sites now known – over 3,000 spots in Europe alone (Bailey et al. 2020) – is an example of how thriving this work is. Underwater archaeology has fought to establish itself as systematic archaeological research. While tensions between commercial salvage firms and archaeologists continue to this day (Martin 2020: 10772), what is more troubling is the sense that sites underwater are not held in the same regard as those on land (Nakagawa 2014). Archaeology underwater is conducted to the same standards as on land and should be held to those same standards, not stricter standards just because a site is submerged. Underwater projects can be evaluated on their ability to ask and answer questions about the past similar to any archaeological project. As this Element demonstrates, the submerged record is global in scale and covers over a million years in time, there is no longer a question of if these sites exist, or if we can investigate them, but rather how will we train future archaeologists to protect and monitor them?

While techniques and technologies are specific to the field, nearly all underwater methods have counterparts or equivalent procedures in terrestrial settings. Archaeologists working on land should welcome the opportunity to learn from and about submerged sites and data, particularly as our approaches and models are likely to be incomplete without a basic understanding of water level fluctuations and how they have impacted human communities across the globe.

While the submerged record is a critical component of world archaeology, it is also threatened by a range of factors; most notably offshore energy development, ocean acidification, warming temperatures, the antiquities trade, and looting. Large-scale offshore renewable energy developments such as wind farms are being proposed at a staggering rate and there is a critical, immediate need for cultural resource managers who are familiar with submerged sites and the basic techniques for finding and investigating them. The investment in wind farms and thus green energy is significant across the globe, including on either side of the Atlantic Ocean and in the North Sea. Ideally, archaeologists and developers can see such projects as an opportunity to work together. Partnerships with industry have been successful in collecting both high-quality and large quantities of data (Gaffney 2022; Gaffney et al. 2009), but data needs to be collected at the scales required for archaeological inquiry. Conversely, while this Element has discussed past sea level rise as a preserver of archaeological sites, current and future sea level rise will have a significant impact on archaeological sites. Modeling has shown that in a sample of nine states in the United States, a 1 m rise will result in the loss of over 13,000 recorded archaeological sites (Anderson et al. 2017). Climate change is impacting the archaeological record both above and below water, as are looting and the buying/selling of artifacts.

Registering and reporting underwater archaeological sites is a critical first step and understanding what to do if waterlogged materials are encountered is critical. As the UNESCO 2001 Convention states, international best practice lists in situ preservation as the first option. Detailed recording, measurements, and mapping can take place fairly quickly and easily, particularly in shallow water. Just as in any other skill, archaeologists should have a familiarity with the policies and procedures for submerged sites as they are becoming more and more likely to encounter material culture underwater in the course of their career. This Element is a good first step in this education and cites many more detailed manuals.

While underwater archaeological sites are essential components of the archaeological record, beyond research they are often the sites of recreation (diving, swimming, snorkeling, boating) and industry (fishing, offshore mineral extraction, offshore wind energy). There are examples of parks and memorials that serve to protect underwater sites and provide educational programs to their communities. For example, the USS *Arizona* Memorial in Pearl Harbor was not created for predominately archaeological reasons, but it attracts more visitors each year than any other underwater site (Maarleveld 2020). Protocols for monitoring other shipwrecks have been implemented while also improving accessibility for recreational diving (e.g., Grenier 1994) and Florida's

Underwater Archaeological Preserves are wonderful examples of the protection of underwater cultural heritage through public archaeology and educational programming (Jameson and Scott-Ireton 2007). Communities living on or near the water are often fascinated by the rich history beneath the waterline and creating opportunities for citizen science, providing accessible field research options, and the creation of maritime heritage trails are very exciting developments in the field (e.g., Lemke et al. 2022; Scott-Ireton et al. 2023). Ultimately, the submerged record will play a vital role in twenty-first-century archaeology. As anthropologists, we can explore deeper (literal and figurative) depths and learn from the long record of human resilience to track some of the most significant changes that occurred in the past.

References

Adovasio, J. M., & Hemmings, A. (2009). *Inner Continental Shelf Archaeology in the Northeast Gulf of Mexico*. Paper presented at the 74th Annual Meeting of the Society for American Archaeology, Atlanta, GA.

Albrectsen, E. (1959). Flinteflækker og frømænd. Odense: *Fynske Minder*.

Alday, C., & Morrisset, S., eds. (2019). Desert archaeology. *Archaeological Review from Cambridge*, **34 (1–205)**.

Amkreutz, L., & van der Vaart-Verschoof, S., eds. (2022). *Doggerland: Lost World under the North Sea*. Leiden: Sidestone Press.

Andersen, S. H. (1980). Tybrind Vig: A preliminary report on a submerged Ertebølle settlement on the Little Belt. *Antikvariske Studier*, **4**: 7–22.

Andersen, S. H. (1987). Tybrind Vig: A submerged Ertebølle settlement in Denmark. In Coles J., & Lawson, A. J., eds. *European Wetlands in Prehistory*. Oxford: Oxford University Press, pp. **253–280**.

Andersen, S. H. (2013). *Tybrind Vig: Submerged Mesolithic Settlements in Denmark*. Jysk Arkæologisk Selskabs Skrifter 77. Arhas: Arhas University Press.

Anderson, D. G., Bissett, T. G., Yerka, S. J. et al. (2017). Sea-level rise and archaeological site destruction: An example from the southeastern United States using DINAA (Digital Index of North American Archaeology). *PLoS ONE*, **12(11): e0188142**.

Anderson, A., Chilczuk, S., Nelson, K., Ruther, R., & Wall-Scheffler, C. (2023). The myth of man the hunter: Women's contribution to the hunt across ethnographic contexts. *PLoS ONE*, **18(6): e0287101**.

Andrews, A. P., & Corletta, R. (1995). A brief history of underwater archaeology in the Maya area. *Ancient Mesoamerica*, **6**: 101–117.

Andrews, E. W. (1959). Dzibilchaltun: Lost city of the Maya. *National Geographic Magazine*, **115(1)**: 90–109.

Ashton, N., Lewis, S. G., De Groote, I., et al. (2014). Hominin footprints from early Pleistocene deposits at Happisburgh, UK. *PLoS ONE*, **9(2)**: e88329.

Astrup, P. M. (2018). *Sea-Level Change in Mesolithic Southern Scandinavia: Long- and Short-Term Effects on Society and the Environment*. Aarhus: Aarhus University Press.

Astrup, P. M., Skriver, C., Benjamin, J., et al. (2019). Underwater shell middens: Excavation and remote sensing of a submerged Mesolithic site at Hjarnø, Denmark. *The Journal of Island and Coastal Archaeology*, **15(4)**: 457–476.

Atherton, M. (2011). *Echoes and Images: The Encyclopedia of Side-Scan and Scanning Sonar Operations*. Vancouver: Oysterlink Publications.

Bailey, G. & King, G. C. P. (2011). Dynamic landscapes and human dispersal patterns: tectonics, coastlines, and the reconstruction of human habitats. *Quaternary Science Reviews*, **30(11–12):1533–1553**.

Bass, G. F. (1964). Underwater excavations at Yassi Ada 1962–1963. *Türk Arkeologji Dergisi*, **20: 40–50**.

Bass, G. F. (1966). *Archaeology under Water*. London: Thames and Hudson.

Bass, G. F. (1971). *Archaeology under Water*. London: Penguin Books.

Bass, G. F. (1972). *A History of Seafaring Based on Underwater Archaeology*. London: Thames and Hudson.

Bass, G. F. (1983). A plea for historical particularism in nautical archaeology. In Gould, R. A., ed. *Shipwreck Anthropology*. Albuquerque: University of New Mexico Press, pp. **91–104**.

Bass, G. F. (1988). *Ships and Shipwrecks of the Americas: A History Based on Underwater Archaeology*. New York: Thames and Hudson.

Bass, G. F., & Van Doorninck, F. H. (1982). *Yassi Ada*. Nautical Archaeology Series, No. 1. College Station: Texas A&M University Press.

Bass, G. F., Throckmorton, P., Du Plat Taylor, J. et al. (1967). Cape Gelidonya: A bronze age shipwreck. *Transactions of the American Philosophical Society*, **57(8): 1–177**.

Bailey, G. N. (2004). The wider significance of submerged archaeological sites and their relevance to world prehistory. In Flemming, N. C., ed. *Submarine Prehistoric Archaeology of the North Sea: Research Priorities and Collaboration with Industry*. CBA Research Report 141. York: Council for British Archaeology, pp. **3–10**.

Bailey, G. N. (2014). New developments in submerged prehistoric archaeology: An overview. In Evans, A. M., Flatman, J. C., &Flemming, N. C., eds. *Prehistoric Archaeology on the Continental Shelf*. New York: Springer, pp. **311–331**.

Bailey, G. N., & Flemming, N. C. (2008). Archaeology of the continental shelf: Marine resources, submerged landscapes and underwater archaeology. *Quaternary Science Reviews*, **27(23): 2153–2165**.

Bailey, G. N., & Parkington, J. (1988). *The Archaeology of Prehistoric Coastlines*. Cambridge: Cambridge University Press.

Bailey, G. N., Harff, J., & Sakellariou, D., eds. (2017). *Under the Sea: Archaeology and Palaeolandscapes of the Continental Shelf*. Cham: Springer.

Bailey, G. N., Galanidou, N., Peeters, H., Jöns, H., & Mennenga, M., eds. (2020). *The Archaeology of Europe's Drowned Landscapes*. Cham: Springer.

Bayón, M. C., & Politis, G. G. (2014). The inter-tidal zone site of La Olla: Early-middle Holocene human adaptation on the Pampean coast of

Argentina. In Evans, A. M., Flatman, J. C., & Flemming, N. C. *Prehistoric Archaeology on the Continental Shelf*. New York: Springer, pp. **115–130**.

Benjamin, J. (2010). Submerged prehistoric landscapes and underwater site discovery: Reevaluating the "Danish model" for international practice. *The Journal of Island and Coastal Archaeology*, **5**: **253–270**.

Benjamin, J., Bonsall, C., Pickard, C., & Fischer, A., eds. (2011). *Submerged Prehistory*. Oxford: Oxbow.

Benjamin, J., O'Leary, M. O., McDonald, J. et al. (2020). Aboriginal artefacts on the continental shelf reveal ancient drowned cultural landscapes in northwest Australia. *PLoS ONE*, **15(7)**: **e0233912**.

Benjamin, J., O'Leary, M. O., McDonald, J. et al. (2023a). Correction: Aboriginal artefacts on the continental shelf reveal ancient drowned cultural landscapes in northwest Australia. *PLoS ONE*, **18(6):e0287490**.

Benjamin, J., O'Leary M. O., McCarthy, J. et al. (2023b). Stone artefacts on the seabed at a submerged freshwater spring can confirm a drowned cultural landscape in Murujuga, Western Australia. *Quaternary Science Reviews*, **313**: **108190**.

Billaud, Y. (2017). Archaeology of underwater caves in France: An overview. In Campbell, P., ed. *The Archaeology of Underwater Caves*. Southampton: Highfield Press, pp. **145–162**.

Björdal, C. G. (2000). *Waterlogged Archaeological Wood: Biodegration and Its Implications for Conservation*. Uppsala: Swedish University of Agricultural Sciences.

Björdal, C. G., Gregory, D., & Trakadas, A., eds. (2012). *WreckProtect: Decay and Protection of Archaeological Wooden Shipwrecks*. Oxford: Archaeopress.

Borhegyi, S. F. (1958). Aqualung archaeology. *Natural History*, **67(3)**: **120–125**.

Borhegyi, S. F. (1959). Underwater archaeology in Guatemala. *Scientific American*, **200(3)**: **100–113**.

Bowens, A. (2008). *Underwater Archaeology: The NAS Guide to Principles and Practice*. 2nd ed. Hoboken: Wiley-Blackwell.

Bradley, R., & Gordon, K. (1988). Human skulls from the River Thames, their dating and significance. *Antiquity*, **62(236)**: **503–509**.

Broadwater, J. D. (2002). Timelines of underwater archaeology. In Barstad, J. F., & Ruppé, C. V., eds. *International Handbook of Underwater Archaeology*. Cham: Springer, pp. **17–24**

Broadwater, J. D. (2023). *A Practical Guide to Maritime Archaeology: With a Focus on the Mid-Atlantic Region*. Richmond: DATA Investigations, LLC.

Bruno, F., Lagudi, A., Gallo, A., et al. (2015). 3D documentation of archeological remains in the underwater park of Baiae. *The International Archives of*

Photogrammetry, Remote Sensing, and Spatial Information Sciences, **XL-5/W5**: **41–46**.

Bruseth, J., ed. (2014). *La Belle: The Ship That Changed History.* College Station: Texas A&M University Press.

Campbell, P. B. (2017). Ritual use of springs and cave lake by Native North American cultures. In Campbell, P., ed. *The Archaeology of Underwater Caves.* Southampton: Highfield Press, pp. **221–250**.

Carabias, D., Cartajena, I., Simmonettii, R., et al. (2014). Submerged paleo-landscapes: Site GNL Quintero 1 (GNLQ1) and the first evidences from the Pacific coast of South America. In Evans, A. M., Flatman, J. C., & Flemming, N. C., eds. *Prehistoric Archaeology on the Continental Shelf.* New York: Springer, pp. **131–150**.

Cavers, M. G., & Henderson, J. C. (2005). Underwater excavation at Ederline Crannog, Loch Awe, Argyll, Scotland. *The International Journal of Nautical Archaeology,* **34(2)**: **282–298**.

Ceruti, M. C. (2023). High-altitude archaeology and the anthropology of sacred mountains: 25 years of explorations and disseminations. In Sarmiento, F. O., ed. *Montology Palimpsest: A Primer of Mountain Geographies.* Cham: Springer, pp. **237–253**.

Chatters, J. C., Kennett, D. J., Asmerom, Y., et al. (2014). Late Pleistocene human skeleton and mtDNA link Paleoamericans and modern Native Americans. *Science,* **344(6185)**: **750–754**.

Chatters, J. C., Rissolo, D., Arroyo Cabrales, J., et al. (2017). Hoyo Negro: tapping the paleoanthropological and paleoecological potential of a deeply submerged underground chamber on the Yucatan Peninsula, Mexico. In Campbell, P., ed. *The Archaeology of Underwater Caves.* Southampton: Highfield Press, pp. **119–130**.

Chang, C.-H., Kaifu, Y., Takai, M., et al. (2015). The first archaic Homo from Taiwan. *Nature Communications,* **6**: **6037**.

Clausen, C. J., Brooks, H. K., & Wesolowsky, A. B. (1975). The early man site at Warm Mineral Springs, Florida. *Journal of Field Archaeology,* **2(3)**: **191–213**.

Clausen, C. J., Cohen, A. D., Emiliani, C., Holman, J. A., & Stipp, J. J. (1979). Little Salt Spring, Florida: A unique underwater site. *Science,* **203(4381)**: **609–614**.

Clottes, J., Courtin, J., & Collina-Girard, J. (2017). The Cosquer cave, Marseilles, France. In Campbell, P., ed. *The Archaeology of Underwater Caves.* Southampton: Highfield Press, pp. **105–118**.

Coggins, C., & Shane, O. C. (1984). *Cenote of Sacrifice: Maya Treasures from the Sacred Well at Chichén Itzá.* Austin: University of Texas Press.

Conrad, G. W., Foster, J. W., Beeker, C. D., & Beland, A. L. (2005). Artefactos de madera recuperados del Manantial de la Aleta, Parque Nacional del Este. *Boletín del Museum del Hombre Dominicano*, **32(39)**: **7–42**.

Cook Hale, J., Benjamin, J., Woo, K., et al. (2021). Submerged landscapes, marine transgression and underwater shell middens: Comparative analysis of site formation and taphonomy in Europe and North America. *Quaternary Science Reviews*, **258**: **106867**.

Delaere, C., & Capriles, J. M. (2020). The context and meaning of an intact Inca underwater offering from Lake Titicaca. *Antiquity*, **94(376)**: **1030–1041**.

Delaere, C., & Warmenbol, E. (2019). The watery way to the world of the dead: Underwater excavations (old and new) at the cave of Han-sur-Lesse, Beligum. In Büster, L., Warmenbol, E., & Mlekuž, D., eds. *Between Worlds: Understanding Ritual Cave Use in Later Prehistory*. Cham: Springer, pp. **137–161**

Delgado, J. (1997). *Encyclopedia of Underwater and Maritime Archaeology*. London: British Museum Press.

Dhony, M. D. K., Adhityatama, S., Triwurjani, R. R., et al. (2023). Underwater archaeology remains in Matano Lake, South of Sulawesi, Indonesia: Evidence of Iron Age Civilization. In *Proceedings of the 2023 Asia Pacific Regional Conference on Underwater Cultural Heritage*. https://apconf .omeka.net/exhibits/show/apconfproceedings/2023.

Ditchfield, K., Ulm, S., Manne, T., et al. (2022). Framing Australian Pleistocene coastal occupation and archaeology. *Quaternary Science Reviews*, **293(1)**: **107706**.

Dixon, J. (1979). *A Predictive Model for the Distribution of Archaeological Sites on the Continental Shelf*. PhD dissertation, Department of Anthropology, Brown University.

Dixon, N. (2004). *The Crannogs of Scotland: An Underwater Archaeology*. Stroud: Tempus.

Doran, G. H., ed. (2002). *Windover: Multidisciplinary Investigations of an Early Archaic Florida Cemetery*. Gainesville: University Press of Florida.

Dortch, J., Beckett, E., Paterson, A., & McDonald, J. (2019). Stone artifacts in the intertidal zone, Dampier Archipelago: Evidence for a submerged coastal site in Northwest Australia. *The Journal of Island and Coastal Archaeology*, **16(2–4)**: **509–523**.

Duggins, R., Price, F. H., Price, M. R., Mollema, I. R., & Puckett, N. (2018). *Manasota Key Offshore: A Prehistoric Cemetery in the Gulf of Mexico*. Paper presented at the Society for Historical and Underwater Archaeology Annual Meeting, New Orleans, LA.

Dunbar, J. S. (1991). Resource orientation of Clovis and Suwannee age Paleoindian sites in Florida. In Bonnichsen, R., & Turnmine, K. L., eds.

Clovis: Origins and Adaptations. College Station: Center for the Study of the First Americans, pp. **185–214**.

Dunbar, J. S., Hemmings, C. A., Vojnovski, P. K., Webb, S. D., & Stanton, W. M. (2006). The Ryan/Harley Site 8JE1004: A Suwannee point site in the Wacissa River, North Florida. In Bonnnichsen, R., Lepper, B. T., Stanford, D., & Waters, M. R., eds. *Paleoamerican Origins: Beyond Clovis*. College Station: Texas A&M University Press, pp. **81–96**.

Dunnavant, J. P. (2021). Have confidence in the sea: Maritime maroons and fugitive geographies. *Antiopde*, **53(3)**: **884–905**.

Easton, N. A., Moore, C., & Mason, A. R. (2021). The archaeology of submerged prehistoric sites on the north coast of North America. *The Journal of Island and Coastal Archaeology*, **16(1)**: **118–149**.

Eitel, K. (2023). Resilience. In Stein, F., ed. *The Open Encyclopedia of Anthropology*. http://doi.org/10.29164/23resilience. www.anthroencyclopedia .com/entry/resilience.

El-Rayis, O. A., Hemeda, E. I., Ismael, A. M., & Jammo, K. (2003). Approaches to environmental restoration of a polluted harbour with submerged archaeology: the Alexandria case study. *Marine Pollution Bulletin*, **47(1–6)**: **193–197**.

Evans, A., Flatman, J. C., & Flemming N. C., eds. (2014). *Prehistoric Archaeology of the Continental Shelf: A Global Review*. New York: Springer.

Evans, A., & Keith, M. E. (2011). Potential contributions of a maritime cultural landscape approach to submerged prehistoric resources, northwestern Gulf of Mexico. In Ford, B., ed. *The Archaeology of Maritime Landscapes*. Cham: Springer, pp. **163–178**.

Evans, A., Russel, M. A., & Leshikar-Denton, M. E. (2010). Local resources, global heritage: An introduction to the 2001 UNESCO Convention on the Protection of the Underwater Cultural Heritage. *Journal of Maritime Archaeology*, **5**: **79–83**.

Faught, M. K. (2002–2004). Submerged Paleoindian and archaic sites of the Big Bend, Florida. *Journal of Field Archaeology*, **29**: **273–290**.

Faught, M. K. (2004). The underwater archaeology of paleolandscapes, Apalachee Bay, Florida. *American Antiquity*, **69**: **235–249**.

Faught, M. K. (2010). The Danish model gets us going: Comment on Jonathan Benjamin's "submerged prehistoric landscapes and underwater site discovery: Reevaluating the 'Danish model' for international practice." *The Journal of Island and Coastal Archaeology*, **5**: **271–273**.

Faught, M. K., & Donoghue, J. F. (1997). Marine inundated archaeological sites and paleofluvial systems: Examples from a karst-controlled continental shelf setting in Apalachee Bay, Northeastern Gulf of Mexico. *Geoarchaeology*, **12(5)**: **417–458**.

Faught, M. K., & Smith, M. F. (2021). The magnificent seven: Marine submerged precontact sites found by systematic geoarchaeology in the Americas. *The Journal of Island and Coastal Archaeology*, **16**(1): **86–102**.

Fedje, D. W., & Josenhans, H. (2000). Drowned forests and archaeology on the continental shelf of British Columbia, Canada. *Geology*, **28**(2): **99–102**.

Fedje, D. W., Wigen, R. J., McClaren, D., & Mackie, Q. (2004). *Pre-Holocene Archaeology and Environment from Karst Caves in Haida Gwaii, West Coast, Canada*. Paper presented at the 57th Annual Northwest Anthropological Conference, Eugene.

Ferguson, L. (1992). *Uncommon Ground: Archaeology and Early African America 1650–1800*. Washington, DC: Smithsonian Institution Press.

Flemming, N. C. (1971). *Cities in the Sea*. New York: Doubleday & Company.

Flemming, N. C. (1980). Structures under water: Apollonia, a model harbor. In Muckelroy, K., ed. *Archaeology under Water: An Atlas of the World's Submerged Sites*. New York: McGraw-Hill, pp. **174–175**.

Flemming, N. C. (2004). *Submarine Prehistoric Archaeology of the North Sea: Research Priorities and Collaboration with Industry*. York: Council for British Archaeology.

Flemming, N. C. (2011). Research infrastructure for systematic study of the prehistoric archaeology of the European submerged continental shelf. In Benjamin, J., Bonsall, C., Pickard, C., & Fischer, A., eds. *Submerged Prehistory*. Oxford: Oxbow, pp. **272–286**.

Flemming, N. C. (2021). *Apollonia on my Mind: The memoir of a paraplegic ocean scientist*. Leiden: Sidestone Press.

Flemming, N. C., Harff, J., Moura, D., Burgess, A., & Bailey, G. N., eds. (2017). *Submerged Landscapes of the European Continental Shelf: Quaternary Paleoenvironments*. Oxford: Wiley.

Fischer, A. (1993b). *Stenalderbopadser på bunden af Smålandsfarvandet. En teori afprøvet ved dykkerbesigtiglse*. *Hørsholm*: Skov-og Naturstyrelsen.

Fischer, A., ed. (1995a). *Man and Sea in the Mesolithic: Coastal Settlement above and below Present Sea Level: Proceedings of the International Symposium, Kalundborg, Denmark 1993*. Oxbow Monograph 53. Oxford: Oxbow.

Fischer, A. (1995b). An entrance to the Mesolithic world below the ocean. Status of ten years' work on the Danish sea floor. In Fischer, A., ed. *Man and Sea in the Mesolithic: Coastal Settlement above and below Present Sea Level: Proceedings of the International Symposium, Kalundborg, Denmark 1993*. Oxbow Monograph 53. Oxford: Oxbow, pp. **371–384**.

Fischer, A. (1997). People and the sea-settlement and fishing along the Mesolithic coasts. In Pedersen, L., Fischer, A., & Aaby, B., eds.

The Danish Storælt since the Ice Age-Man, Sea and Forest. Oxford: Oxbow, pp. **63–77**.

Fischer, A. (2007). Coastal fishing in Stone Age Denmark – evidence from below and above the present sea-level and from the bones of human beings. In Milner, N., Craig, O. E., & Bailey, G. N., eds. *Shell Middens and Coastal Resources along the Atlantic Façade, Held in York September 2005.* Oxford: Oxbow, pp. **54–69**.

Ford, B., Halligan, J., & Catsambis, A. (2020). *Our Blue Plant: An Introduction to Maritime and Underwater Archaeology.* Oxford: Oxford University Press.

Gaffney, V. (2022). Forward. In Amkreutz, L., & van der Vaart-Verschoof, S., eds. *Doggerland: Lost World under the North Sea.* Leiden: Sidestone Press, pp. **7–8**.

Gaffney, V., & Fitch, S., eds. (2022). *Europe's Lost Frontiers: Volume I Context and Methodology.* Oxford: Archaeopress.

Gaffney, V., Fitch, S., & Smith, D. (2009). *Europe's Lost World: The Discovery of Doggerland.* York: Council for British Archaeology.

Galili, E., Benjamin, J., Eshed, V., et al. (2019). A submerged 7000-year-old village and seawall demonstrated earliest known coastal defence against sea-level rise. *PLoS ONE,* **14(12): e0222560**.

Galili, E., & Wienstein-Evron, M. (1985). Prehistory and paleoenvironments of submerged sites along the Carmel coast of Israel. *Paleobiology,* **11: 37–52**.

Galili, E., Weinstien-Evron, M., Hershkovitz, I., et al. (1993). Atlit-Yam: A prehistoric site on the sea floor off the Israeli coast. *Journal of Field Archaeology,* **20(2): 133–157**.

Garrison, E., & Cook Hale, J. (2021). "The early days" – underwater prehistoric archaeology in the USA and Canada. *The Journal of Island and Coastal Archaeology,* **16(1): 27–45**.

Garrison, E., Cook Hale, J., Cameron, C. S., & Smith, E. (2016). The archaeology, sedimentology and paleontology of Gray's Reef National Marine Sanctuary and nearby hard bottom reefs along the mid continental shelf of the Georgia Bight. *Journal of Archaeological Science: Reports,* **5: 240–262**.

Gaspari, A., Miran, E., & Bostjan, O. (2011). A Palaeolithic wooden point from Ljubljansko Barje, Solvenia. In Benjamin, J., Bonsall, C., Pickard, C., & Fischer, A., eds. *Submerged Prehistory.* Oxford: Oxbrow Books, pp. **186–192**.

Gifford, J. A, Koski, S. H., Newsom, L. A., & Milideo, L. (2017). Little Salt Spring: Excavations on the 27-meter ledge, 2008–2011. In Campbell, P., ed. *The Archaeology of Underwater Caves.* Southampton: Highfield Press, pp. **73–104**.

Green, J. (2016). *Maritime Archaeology: A Technical Handbook*. Second edition. London: Routledge.

Grenier, R. (1994). The concept of the Louisbourg Underwater Museum. *The Northern Mariner/Le Marin du nord*, **IV(2)**: **3–10**.

Gregory, D., & Mattiesen, H., eds. (2012). Preserving archaeological materials *in Situ* (Paris4). *Conservation and Management of Archaeological Sites*, **14**: **1–4**.

Grier, C., Kim, J., & Uchiyama, J., eds. (2006). *Beyond Affluent-foragers: Rethinking Hunter-Gatherer Complexity*. Oxford: Oxbow.

Goggin, J. M. (1960). Underwater archaeology: Its nature and limitations. *American Antiquity*, **25(3)**: **348–354**.

Gómez Otero, J. (2007). *Dieta, Uso del Espacio y Evolución en Poblaciones Cazadoras-Recolectoras de la Costa Centro – septentrional de Patagonia Durante el Holoceno Medio y Tardío*. PhD dissertation, Facultad de Filosofía y Letras, Universidad Buenos Aires.

Gould, R. (1983). *Shipwreck Anthropology*. Albuquerque: University of New Mexico Press.

Gould, R. (2000). *Archaeology and the Social History of Ships*. Cambridge: Cambridge University Press.

Grøn, O., Boldreel, L. O., Hermand, J. P. et al. (2018). Detecting human-knapped flint with marine high-resolution reflection seismics: A preliminary study of new possibilities for subsea mapping of submerged Stone Age sites. *Underwater Technology*, **35(2)**: **35–49**.

Grøn, O., Boldreel, L. O., Smith, M. F. et al. (2021). Acoustic mapping of submerged Stone Age sites—a Hald approach. *Remote Sensing*, **13(3)**: **445**.

Guilderson, T. P., Burckle, L., Hemmings, S., & Peltier, W. R. (2000). Late Pleistocene sea level variations derived from the Argentine shelf. *Geochemistry, Geophysics, Geosystems: An Electronic Journal of Earth Sciences*, **1**: **200GC000098**.

Gusick, A., Maloney, J., King, R. B., & Braje, T. J. (2019). *Emerging Technologies in the Search for Submerged Cultural Landscapes of the Pacific Continental Shelf*. Paper presented at the Offshore Technology Conference, Houston, Texas, May 2019. OTC-29221-MS.

Habu, J., Matsui, A., Yamamoto, A., & Kanno, T. (2011). Shell midden archaeology in Japan: Aquatic food acquisition and long-term change in the Jomon culture. *Quaternary International*, **239(1–2)**: **19–27**.

Halligan, J. J., Waters, M. R., Perrotti, A. et al. (2016). Pre-Clovis occupation 14,550 years ago at the Page-Ladson site, Florida, and the peopling of the Americas. *Science Advances*, **2(5)**: **1–8**.

Hamilton, D. L. (1976). *Conservation of Metal Objects from Underwater Sites: A Study in Methods*. Austin: Texas Antiquities Committee Publication No. 1.

Hamilton, D. L. (1984). Preliminary report on the archaeological investigations of the submerged remains of Port Royal, Jamaica 1981–1982. *International Journal of Nautical Archaeology and Underwater Exploration*, **13**(1):**11–25**.

Hamilton, D. L. (1996). *Basic Methods of Conserving Underwater Archaeological Material Culture*. Washington, DC: Legacy Resource Management Program, United States Department of Defense.

Hamilton, D. L. (1999). *Methods for Conserving Archaeological Materials from Underwater Sites*. College Station: Conservation Research Laboratory, Center for Maritime Archaeology and Conservation Texas A&M University.

Hamilton, D. L. (2006). Port Royal, Jamaica: Archaeological past and development potential. *Underwater Cultural Heritage at Risk*, **49–51**.

Harding, A., Cadogan, G., & Howell, R. (1969). Pavlopetri, an underwater bronze age town in Laconia. *The Annual of the British School at Athens*, **64**: **113–142**.

Hayashida, K., Kimura, J., & Sasaki, R. (2014). State and perspectives of submerged sites in Japan. In Evans, A., Flatman, J. C., & Flemming N. C., eds. *Prehistoric Archaeology of the Continental Shelf: A Global Review*. New York: Springer, pp. **275–290**.

Hermand, J. P., Grøn, O., Asch, M., & Ren, Q. Y. (2011). Modelling flint acoustics for detection of submerged Stone Age sites. In *Proceedings of OCEANS 2011 IEEE Conference*, Santander, Spain, pp. **1–9**. https://ieeex plore.ieee.org/document/6107308.

Hoffman, C. A. (1983). A Mammoth kill site in the Silver Springs Run. *The Florida Anthropologist*, **36**(**1–2**): **83–87**.

Hublin, J-J., Weston, D., Gunz, P., et al. (2009). Out of the North Sea: The Zeeland Ridges Neandertal. *Journal of Human Evolution*, **57**(**6**): **777–785**.

Iba, I. (2005). The Awazu site, a shell midden on the bottom of Lake Biwa, Japan. *Journal of Wetland Archaeology*, **5**(**1**): **35–48**.

Irwanto, D. (2019). *Sundaland: Tracing the Cradle of Civilizations*. West Java: Indonesia Hydro Media.

Jameson, J. H., & Scott-Ireton, D. A., eds. (2007). *Out of the Blue: Public Interpretation of Maritime Cultural Resources*. New York: Springer.

Jasinski, M., & Warmenbol, E. (2017). The *Trou de Han* in Han-Sur-Lesse, Belgium. In Campbell, P., ed. *The Archaeology of Underwater Caves*. Southampton: Highfield Press, pp. **163–184**.

Jerbic, K. (2020). *Zambratija: A 6,000-Year-Old Pile-dwelling Submerged under the Adriatic Sea*. Unpublished PhD dissertation, Flinders University, Adelaide.

Johnson, L. L., & Stright, M. (1992). *Paleoshorelines and Prehistory: An Investigation of Method*. Baca Raton: CRC Press.

Josenhans, H. W., Fedje, D. W., Conway, K. W., & Barrie, J. V. (1995). Post glacial sea levels on the western Canadian continental shelf: Evidence for rapid change, extensive subaerial exposure, and early human habitation. *Marine Geology*, **125**: **73–94**.

Josenhans, H. W., Fedje, D. W, Pienitz, R., & Southon, J. (1997). Early humans and rapidly changing Holocene sea-levels in the Queen Charlotte Islands – Hecate Strait, British Columbia. *Science*, **277**: **71–72**.

Keith, M. E. (2016). *Site Formation Processes of Submerged Shipwrecks*. Gainesville: University Press of Florida.

Khalil, E., & Mustafa, M. (2002). Underwater archaeology in Egypt. In Ruppe, C. V., & Barstad, J. F., eds. *International Handbook of Underwater Archaeology*. Cham: Springer, pp. **519–534**.

Kinkella, A., & Lucero, L. J. (2017). Actun Ek Nen: Relfections on the Black Mirror Cave at the Cara Blanca Pools, Belize. In Campbell, P., ed. *The Archaeology of Underwater Caves*. Southampton: Highfield Press, pp. **185–200**.

Klyuev, M., Schreider, A., & Rakitin, I., eds. (2023). *Technical Means for Underwater Archaeology*. Cham: Springer.

Lambeck, K., Esat, T. M., & Potter, E.-K. (2002). Links between climate and sea levels for the past three million years. *Nature*, **419(6903)**: **199–206**.

Lawrence, G. F. (1929). Antiquities from the middle Thames. *Archaeological Journal*, **86(1)**: **69–98**.

Leineweber. R., Lubke, H., Hellmund, M., Dohle, H.-J., & Kloob, S. (2011). A late Neolithic fishing fence in Lake Arendsee, Sachsen-Anhalt, Germany. In Benjamin, J., Bonsall, C., Pickard, C., & Fischer, A., eds. *Submerged Prehistory*. Oxford: Oxbrow Books, pp. **173–185**.

Lemke, A. (2015). Great Lakes Rangifer and Paleoindians: Archaeological and paleontological caribou remains from Michigan. *PaleoAmerica*, **1(3)**: **276–283**.

Lemke, A. (2016). *Anthropological Archaeology Underwater: Hunting Architecture and Foraging Lifeways beneath the Great Lakes*. PhD Dissertation, Department of Anthropology, University of Michigan, Ann Arbor.

Lemke, A., ed. (2018). *Foraging in the Past: Archaeological Studies of Hunter-Gatherer Diversity*. Denver: University Press of Colorado.

Lemke, A. (2021a). Submerged prehistory and anthropological archaeology: Do underwater studies contribute to theory? *Journal of Island and Coastal Archaeology*, **16(1)**: **5–26**.

Lemke, A. (2021b). Literal niche construction: Built environments of hunter-gatherers and hunting architecture. *Journal of Anthropological Archaeology*, **62**: **101276**.

Lemke, A. (2022). *The Architecture of Hunting: The Built Environment of Hunter-Gatherers and Its Impact on Mobility, Property, Leadership, and Labor.* College Station: Texas A&M University Press.

Lemke, A., Grinnan, N., & Haigler, J. (2022). Getting your feet wet: Barriers to inclusivity in underwater archaeology and how to break them. *Advances in Archaeological Practice*, **10(2)**: **129–139**.

Lemke, A., & O'Shea, J. (2022). Drowning the Pompeii premise: Frozen moments, single events, and the character of submerged archaeological sites. *World Archaeology*, **54(1)**: **142–156**.

Lemke, A., O'Shea, J., Reynolds, R., & Palazzolo, T. (2023). *Virtual Worlds: Underwater Archaeology and Indigenous Engagement.* Paper presented at the 88th Society for American Archaeology Annual Meeting, Portland, Oregon.

Lenihan, D. J., Cockrell, W. A, & Murphy, L. E. (2017). How underwater archaeology brought light to darkness in the American karst. In Campbell, P., ed. *The Archaeology of Underwater Caves*. Southampton: Highfield Press, pp. **44–72**.

Leshikar, M. E. (1988). The earliest watercraft: From rafts to Viking ships. In Bass, G. F., ed. *Shipwrecks of the Americas: A History Based on Underwater Archaeology*. New York: Thames and Hudson, pp. **13–32**.

Lisiecki, L. E., & Raymo, M. E. (2005). A Pliocene-Pleistocene stack of 57 globally distributed benthic Delta O-18 records. *Paleoceanography*, **20(1)**: PA1003.

Long, D., Wickham-Jones, C. R., & Ruckley, N.A. (1986). A flint artefact from the northern North Sea. In Roe, D. A., ed. *Studies in the Upper Palaeolithic of Britain and Northwest Europe*, British Archaeological Reports International Series 296. Oxford: BAR Publishing, pp. **55–62**.

Lovis, W. A., Arbogast, A. F., & Monaghan, W. C. (2012). *The Geoarchaeology of Lake Michigan Coastal Dunes*. Lansing: Michigan State University Press.

Luna Erreguerena, P. (1989). Underwater archaeology in Mexico. In Arnold, J. B., ed. *Underwater Archaeology Proceedings of the Society for Historical Archaeology Conference*. Tucson: Society for Historical Archaeology, pp. **149–151**.

Maarleveld, T. J. (2020). Underwater sites in archaeological conservation and preservation. In Smith C., ed. *Encyclopedia of Global Archaeology*. Cham: Springer, pp. **10795–10802**.

MacDonald, B. L., Chatters, J. C., Reinhardt, E. G., et al., (2020). Paleoindian ochre mines in the submerged caves of the Yucatán Peninsula, Quintana Roo, Mexico. *Science Advances*, **6: eaba1219.**

Mahon, I., Pizarro, O., Johnson-Roberson, M., et al. (2011). Reconstructing Pavlopetri: Mapping the world's oldest submerged town using stereo-vision. In *2011 IEEE International Conference on Robotics and Automation*, Shanghai, China, pp. **2315–2321**. https://ieeexplore.ieee.org/document/5980536.

Malm, T. (1995). Excavating submerged Stone Age sites in Denmark – the Tybrind Vig example. In Fischer, A., ed. *Man & Sea in the Mesolithic: Coastal Settlement above and below Present Sea Level*. Oxbow Monographs No. 53. New York: Dan Brown Book Company, pp. **385–396.**

Martin, C. J. M. (2020). Underwater archaeology. In Smith C., ed. *Encyclopedia of Global Archaeology*. Cham: Springer, pp. **10771–10781**

Marden, L. (1959). Up from the well of time. *National Geographic Magazine*, **115(1): 110–129.**

Masters, P. M., & Flemming, N. C., eds. (1983). *Quaternary Coastlines and Marine Archaeology: Towards the Prehistory of Land Bridges and Continental Shelves*. London: Academic Press.

Maus, M., Conrad, G., Foster, J., & Beeker, C. (2017). Underwater caves in the Taíno world. In Campbell, P., ed. *The Archaeology of Underwater Caves*. Southampton: Highfield Press, pp. **201–220.**

Mazurkevich, A., & Dolbunova, E. (2011). Underwater investigations in north-west Russia: Lacustrine archaeology of Neolithic pile dwellings. In Benjamin, J., Bonsall, C., Pickard, C., & Fischer, A., eds. *Submerged Prehistory*. Oxford: Oxbow, pp. **158–172.**

McCarthy, J., & Benjamin, J. (2014). Multi-image photogrammetry for underwater archaeological site recording: An accessible, diver-based approach. *Journal of Maritime Archaeology*, **9(1): 95–114.**

McKillop, H. (2005). Finds in Belize document Late Classic Maya salt making and Canoe Transport. *Proceedings of the National Academy of Sciences*, **102 (15): 5630–5634.**

McKinnon, J., Roth, M. J., & Carrell, T. L. (2020). *Submerged Battlefield Survey Manual: American Battlefield Protection*. Santa Fe: Ships of Exploration and Discovery.

Memet, J. B. (2008). Conservation of underwater cultural heritage: Characteristics and new technologies in underwater cultural heritage. *Museum International*, **240: 42–49.**

Missiaen, T., Sakellariou, D., & Flemming, N. C. (2017). Survey strategies and techniques in underwater geoarchaeological reseach: An overview with emphasis on prehistoric sites. In Bailey G. N., Jan H. & Sakellariou D., eds. *Under the Sea: Archaeology and Palaeolandscapes of the Continental Shelf.* Cham: Springer, pp. **21–37**.

Momber, G. (2000). Drowned and deserted: A submerged prehistoric landscape in the Solent. *International Journal of Nautical Archaeology,* **29**(1): **86–99**.

Momber, G., Tomalin, D., Scife, R., Satchell, J., & Gillespie, J., eds. (2011). *Mesolithic Occupation at Bouldnor Cliff and the Submerged Prehistorical Landscapes of the Solent.* York: Council for British Archaeology.

Monteleone, K. (2013). *Lost Worlds: Locating Submerged Archaeological Sites in Southeast Alaska.* PhD Dissertation, Department of Anthropology, University of New Mexico, Albuquerque.

Monteleone, K., Thompson, A. E., & Keith, P. M. (2021). Virtual cultural landscapes: Geospatial visualization of past environments. *Archaeological Prospection,* **28**: **379–401**.

Morris, M. A., Krysl, P., Rivera-Collazo, I. C., & Hildebrand, J. A. (2022). The resonant acoustic signatures of lithic debitage. *Journal of Archaeological Science: Reports,* **41**: **103266**.

Morrison, I. (1985). *Landscape with Lake Dwellings.* Edinburgh: Edinburgh University Press.

Mortensen, M. N., Egsgaard, H., Hvilsed, S., Shashoua, Y., & Glastrup, J. (2007). Characterisation of the polyethylene glycol impregnation of the Swedish warship Vasa and one of the Danish Skuldelev Viking ship. *Journal of Archaeological Science,* **34**: **1211–1218**.

Muckelroy, K. (1978). *Maritime Archaeology.* Cambridge: Cambridge University Press.

Muckelroy, K., ed. (1980). *Archaeology under Water: An Atlas of the World's Submerged Sites.* New York: McGraw-Hill.

Müller, S. (1897). Vor Oldtid: Danmarks forhistoriske archæology. Denmark: Nabu Press.

Nakagawa, H. (2014). *Submerged Archaeological Sites in the Lake Biwa, Japan.* Paper presented at the Asia Pacific Conference on Underwater Archaeology, Hawaii.

Olsen, O., & Crumlin-Pedersen, O. (1968). The Skuldelev Ships: A Report of the Final Underwater Excavation in 1959 and Salvaging Operation in 1962. *Acta Archaeologica.* Hoboken: Wiley Blackwell Publishing

O'Shea, J. M. (2002). The archaeology of scattered wreck-sites: Formation processes and shallow water archaeology in western Lake Huron. *The International Journal of Nautical Archaeology,* **31**(2): **211–227**.

O'Shea, J. M. (2015). Strategies and techniques for the discovery of submerged sites on the Alpena-Amberley Ridge. In Sonnenburg E., Lemke, A. K., &

O'Shea, J. M., eds. *Caribou Hunting in the Upper Great Lakes: Archaeological, Ethnographic, and Paleoenvironmental Perspectives*. Ann Arbor: University of Michigan, pp. **105–114**.

O'Shea, J. M. (2021). Mirco-regional approaches for submerged site archaeology. *The Journal of Island and Coastal Archaeology*, **16(1)**: **103–117**.

O'Shea, J. M. (2023). *Submerged Prehistory in the Americas: Methods, Approaches, and Results*. New York: Routledge.

O'Shea, J. M., & Lemke, A. (2020). A layered approach for the discovery and mapping of prehistoric sites beneath Lake Huron. *Marine Technology Society Journal*, **54(3)**: **23–32**.

O'Shea, J. M., Lemke, A. K., Nash, B. S., et al. (2021). Central Oregon obsidian from a submerged early Holocene archaeological site beneath Lake Huron. *PLOS ONE*, **16(5)**: **e0250840**.

O'Shea, J. M., Lemke, A. K., Sonnenburg, E., Reynolds, R. G., & Abbot, B. (2014). A 9,000-year-old caribou hunting structure beneath Lake Huron. *PNAS*, **111(19)**: **6911–6915**.

O'Shea, J. M., & Meadows, G. A. (2009). Evidence for early hunters beneath the Great Lakes. *PNAS*, **106(25)**: **10120–10123**.

Palazzolo, T., Lemke, A., Zhang, C., et al. (2021). DeepDive: The use of virtual worlds to create an ethnography of an ancient civilization. In Stephanidis, C., Harris, D., Li, W. –C., et al., eds. *HCI International 2021 – Late Breaking Papers: Cognition, Inclusion, Learning and Culture*. Cham: Springer, pp. **615–629**.

Pearson, C. (1987). *Conservation of Marine Archaeological Objects*. London: Butterworths.

Perttula, T., Iruegas, S. A., & Ellis, G. L. (1966). *An Assessment of the Threatened Prehistoric and Historic Archaeological Resources at Falcon Reservoir, Zapata and Starr Counties, Texas*. Cultural Resource Management Report 9. Division of Antiquities Protection, Texas Historical Commission, Austin.

Plets, R., Dix, J., Bastos, A., & Best, A. (2007). Characterization of buried inundated peat on seismic (Chirp) data, inferred from core information. *Archaeological Prospection*, **14**: **261–272**.

Piña Chan, R. (1968). *Jaina: La cases en el agua*. Mexico: Intituto Nacional de Antropología e Historia.

Puckett, N. (2021). Combining underwater and terrestrial research approaches in the Great Basin Desert, Walker Lake, Nevada. *The Journal of Island and Coastal Archaeology*, **16(1)**: **64–85**.

Pullen, D. (2013). The life and death of a Mycenaean port town: Kalamianos on the Saronic Gulf. *Journal of Maritime Archaeology*, **8**: **245–262**.

Purdy, B. (1988). *Wet Site Archaeology*. Cald-Well: Telford Press.

Ren, Q. Y., Grøn, O., & Hermand, J. P. (2011). On the in-situ detection of flint for underwater Stone Age archaeology. In *Proceedings of OCEANS 2011 IEEE Conference*, Santander, Spain, pp. 1–7. https://ieeexplore.ieee.org/abstract/document/6003529.

Richards, V., & McKinnon, J. (2010). *In Situ Conservation of Cultural Heritage: Public, Professionals, and Preservation*. Adelaide: Flinders Program in Maritime Archaeology.

Rissolo, D., Arce, R. C., Jaskolski, C., Erreguerena, P. L., & Chatters, J. C. (2015). Novel application of 3D documentation techniques at a submerged Late Pleistocene cave site in Quintana Roo, Mexico. In *2015 Digital Heritage*, Granada, Spain: IEEE, pp. 181–182. https://doi.org/10.1109/DigitalHeritage.2015.7413868.

Robinson, D., & Goddio F. (2015). *Thonis-Heracleion in Context*. Oxford Centre for Maritime Archaeology Monograph 8. Oxford: School of Archaeology, University of Oxford.

Rowland, M. J., & Ulm, S. (2011). Indigenous fish traps and weirs of Queensland. *Queensland Archaeological Research*, **14**: 1–58.

Rowley-Conwy, P., ed. (1999). Arctic Archaeology. *World Archaeology*, **33(3): 1–180.**

Saad, S., Palazzolo, T., Zhang, C., et al. (2022). Learning to evolve procedural content in games using cultural algorithms. In *Fourth International Conference on Transdisplinary Artificial Intelligence, IEEE*, pp. **106–115**. https://ieeexplore.ieee.org/document/9951556.

Sakellariou, D., Rousakis, G., Maroulakis, S., et al. (2011). *The Submerged City of Pavlopetri*. In Poseidons Reich XVI, (DEGUWA 2011), Heidelberg, 18–20 February 2011.

Schiltmans, D. (2022). Rotterdam-Yangtze harbour: Excavating at 20 meters deep. In Amkreutz, L., & van der Vaart-Verschoof, S., eds. *Doggerland: Lost World under the North Sea*. Leiden: Sidestone Press, pp. **119–123**.

Scott-Ireton, D., Jones, Jennifer E., & Raupp, J. T. (2023). *Citizen Science in Maritime Archaeology: The Power of Public Engagement*. Gaineville: University Press of Florida.

Scuvée, F., & Vérague, J. (1988). Le gisement sous marin du Paléolithique Moyen de l'Anse de la Mondrée à Fermanville (Manche). Cherbourg: LITTUS-C.E.H.P.

Shih, P. T.-Y., Chen, Y.-H., & Chen, J.-C. (2013). Historic shipwreck study in Dongsha Atoll with bathymetric LiDAR. *Archaeological Prospection*, **21(2): 139–146.**

Skaarup, J. (1983). Submarine Stenalderbopladser I Det Sydfynske Øhav. Antikvariske Studier 6, Fredningsstyrelsen, Copenhagen.

Skaarup, J. (1993). Submerged Settlements. In Hvass, S., & Storgaard, B., eds. *Digging into the Past: 25 Years of Archaeology in Denmark*. Aarhus: Aarhus University Press.

Smith, M. (2020). Geoarchaeological investigations at the Ryan-Harley Paleoindian Site, Florida (8JE1004): Implications for human settlement of the Wicissa River Basin during the Younger Dryas. *Geoarchaeology*, **35**(4): **451–466**.

Smith, M. (2022). Geoarchaeological excavations at the Guest Mammoth Site (8MR130), Florida, USA. *Quaternary Science Reviews*, **279**: **107385**.

Smith, M., Joy, S. A., Halligan, J. J. et al. (2022). Liquid landscapes: The contributions of a new wave of submerged prehistoric archaeology to the Paleoindian and early archaic record of the southeast United States. In Miller, S., Smallwood, A., & Tune, J., eds. *The American Southeast of the End of the Ice Age*. Tuscaloosa: University of Alabama Press, pp. **213–229**.

Sonnenburg, E. P., & O'Shea, J. M. (2017). Archaeological landscapes during the 10–8 ka Lake Stanley Lowstand on the Alpena-Amberley Ridge, Lake Huron. *Geoarchaeology*, **32**(2): **230–247**.

Sonnenburg, E. P., Boyce, J. I., & Reinhardt, E. G. (2011). Quartz flakes in lakes: Mircodebitage evidence for submerged Great Lakes prehistoric (Late Paleoindian-Early Archaic) tool-making sites. *Geology*, **39**(7): **631–634**.

Stead, I. M. (1985). *The Battersea Shield*. London: British Museum Publications.

Stickel, G. E., & Garrison, E. G. (1988). New applications of remote sensing: Geophysical prospection for underwater archaeological sites in Switzerland. In Purdy, B., ed. *Wet Site Archaeology*. Cald-Well: Telford Press, pp. **69–88**.

Thompson, V. D. (2022). Considering ideas of collective action, institutions, and "hunter-gatherers" in the American southeast. *Journal of Archaeological Research*, **31**: **503–560**. https://doi.org/10.1007/s10814-022-09179-3.

Throckmorton, P. (1970). *Shipwrecks and Archaeology: The Unharvested Sea*. Boston: Little Brown & Company.

Veth, P., Smith, M., & Hiscock, P. (2005). *Desert Peoples: Archaeological Perspectives*. Malden: Blackwell.

Wakefield, S., Grove, K., & Chandler, D. (2020). Introduction. In Chandler, D., Grove, K., & Wakefield, S., eds. *Resilience in the Anthropocene*. London: Routledge, pp. **1–21**.

Ward, I., Bastos, A., Carabias, D., et al. (2022). Submerged palaeolandscapes of the southern hemisphere (SPLOSH) – what is emerging from the southern hemisphere. *World Archaeology*, **54**(1): **6–28**.

Webb, D. S. (2006). *First Floridians and Last Mastodons: The Page-Ladson Site in the Aucilla River*. New York: Springer.

Werz, B. E. J. S., & Flemming, N. C. (2001). Discovery in Table Bay of the oldest handaxes yet found underwater demonstrates preservation of hominid artefacts on the continental shelf. *South African Journal of Science*, **97**: **183–185**.

Westley, K., Bell, R., Pelts, R., & Quinn, R. (2011). Investigating submerged archaeological landscapes: A research strategy illustrated with case studies from Ireland and Newfoundland, Canada. In Benjamin, J., Bonsall, C., Pickard, C., & Fischer, A., eds. *Submerged Prehistory*. Oxford: Oxbrow Books, pp. **129–144**.

Whitehead, H. W., & Lickliter-Mundon, M. (2023). *Strides toward Standard Methodologies in Aeronautical Archaeology*. Cham: Springer.

Willerslev, R. (2009). Hunting the elk by imitating the reindeer: A critical approach to ecological anthropology and the problems of adaptation and resilience among hunter-gatherers. In Hastrup, K., ed. *The Question of Resilience: Social Responses to Climate Change*. Copenhagen: The Royal Danish Academy of Sciences and Letters, pp. **271–292**.

Willey, G. R., & Phillips, P. (1958). *Method and Theory in American Archaeology*. Chicago: The University of Chicago Press.

Wiseman, C., O'Leary, M. O., Hacker, J., et al. (2021). A multi-scalar approach to marine survey and underwater archaeological site prospection in Murujuga, Western Australia. *Quaternary International*, **584**: **152–170**.

York, J. (2002). The life cycle of bronze age metalwork from the Thames. *Oxford Journal of Archaeology*, **21(1)**: **77–92**.

Zant, C., Skibo, J., Rosebrough, A., & Thomsen, T. (2023). *What's Canoe with you? Understanding Wisconsin's Inland Prehistoric Maritime Landscapes*. Paper presented at the 56th Annual Conference of Historical and Underwater Archaeology, Lisbon, Portugal.

Acknowledgments

Many thanks to Michael Galaty for the invitation to write this manuscript, and to the Series editorial team Eli Dollarhide, Junko Habu, John K. Millhauser, Patricia A. McAnanay, and Rita Wright. I greatly enjoyed the project, particularly learning more about the world-class archaeology taking place below water. I truly appreciate the careful reading and review provided by the editorial team and anonymous reviewers as well as the detailed copyediting completed by Kathie Uttech Gordon. My sincere appreciation goes to Morgan F. Smith, Jonathan Benjamin, Garry Momber, Kelly Monteleone, and Sam Meacham for supplying wonderful images. My dearest friends, colleagues, and Captain John O'Shea have been the highlight of my underwater career, including Tyler Schultz, Robert Reynolds, Guy Meadows, Lisa Sonnenburg, and many others. One can never thank or appreciate Lake Huron enough for her majesty and unique spirit, but I am very grateful for the gorgeous vistas she provided during the writing of this manuscript.

Anthropological Archaeology in the 21st Century

Eli Dollarhide

New York University Abu Dhabi

Eli Dollarhide is an archaeological anthropologist who specializes in the prehistory of the Middle East with a focus on the Persian Gulf. His research investigates the role of small and rural settlements in the development of Bronze Age exchange networks and political systems. Dollarhide co-directs research at the UNESCO World Heritage Site of Bat, Oman and investigates ancient ceramic technologies. See: https://nyuad.nyu.edu/en/research/faculty-labs-and-projects/humanities-research-fellowship-program/research-fellows/eli-dollarhide.html.

Michael Galaty

University of Michigan

Michael Galaty is Professor of Anthropology in the Department of Anthropology and Director and Curator of European and Mediterranean Archaeology in the Museum of Anthropological Archaeology at the University of Michigan. He conducts fieldwork in Albania, Greece, and Kosovo, with a focus on the prehistoric origins of social inequalities. To that end, he utilizes intensive regional survey and targeted excavations, along with various laboratory techniques, to track the changing economic and political factors that lead to transformative changes in Mediterranean and Balkan social systems, during the Bronze Age, in particular.

Junko Habu

University of California, Berkeley

Junko Habu is Professor of Anthropology and Chair of the Center for Japanese Studies, University of California, Berkeley, and Affiliate Professor of the Research Institute for Humanity and Nature. She has published extensively on Japanese and East Asian archaeology, hunter-gatherer archaeology and historical ecology. Her current research focuses on the intersection of archeology, agroecology and traditional ecological knowledge to consider the resilience of socioeconomic systems in the past, present and future. For more information, see https://junkohabu.com/

Patricia A. McAnany

University of North Carolina at Chapel Hill

Patricia A. McAnany, Kenan Eminent Professor and Chair of Anthropology at the University of North Carolina at Chapel Hill, is co-director of Proyecto Arqueológico Colaborativo del Oriente de Yucatán – a community-archaeology project at Tahcabo, Yucatán, México. She co-founded and directs InHerit: Indigenous Heritage Passed to Present (www.in-herit.org) a UNC program that generates collaborative research and education projects focused on archaeology and cultural heritage with communities in the Maya region and North Carolina. She is the author of several books (most recently Maya Cultural Heritage: How Archaeologists and Indigenous Peoples Engage the Past) as well as journal articles and book chapters on a range of archaeological and heritage topics.

John K. Millhauser

North Carolina State University

John K. Millhauser is an Associate Professor of Anthropology in the Department of Sociology and Anthropology at North Carolina State University. His archaeological work in Mexico centers on rural communities and social economies under Mexica and Spanish rule. His current research integrates economic anthropology and political ecology to better understand the origins of poverty and structural violence. For more information, visit chass.ncsu.edu/people/jkmillha/

Rita Wright

New York University

Rita Wright, Professor Emerita of Anthropology at New York University. Using Near Eastern texts as secondary sources and ancient technologies (ceramics and weaving), she investigates divisions of labor and women's contributions to history. In the field she has conducted research in Afghanistan, Pakistan, and Iran, predominately in Baluchistan at Mehrgarh and the Punjab, Pakistan, at the city of Harappa. Her Landscape and Settlement survey of Harappa's rural areas is the first conducted in studies of the Indus civilization. She is founder and editor of Cambridge University Press, Case Studies in Early Societies, especially Ancient Indus: Urbanism, Economy, and Society (Cambridge University Press, 2010)

About the Series

This Element offers anthropological and contemporary perspectives in the study of prehistoric and historic societies globally and cutting-edge research with balanced coverage of well-known sites and understudied times and places. We solicit contributions based on three themes: 1. new methods and technologies producing fresh understandings of the past; 2. theoretical approaches challenging basic concepts and offering new insights; 3. archaeological responses for the 21st century providing informed choices for the present. Individual volumes focus on specific sites and regions that highlight the diversity of human experience around the world and across history which include scholars working throughout North America, Mesoamerica, Europe and the Mediterranean, Africa, the Middle East, and South and East Asia and readers with an avid interest in the latest frontiers in archaeological thought. The media-rich volumes will be an important resource for students, scholars.